A PRACTICAL GUIDE TO
Assessing English Language Learners

Christine Coombe
Dubai Men's College

Keith Folse
University of Central Florida

Nancy Hubley
Independent Consultant and Materials Writer

Ann Arbor
The University of Michigan Press

Published in the United States of America
The University of Michigan Press
Manufactured in the United States of America

∞ Printed on acid-free paper

2017   2016   2015   2014   7   6   5   4

ISBN-13: 978-0-472-03201-3

Library of Congress Cataloging-in-Publication Data

Coombe, Christine A. (Christine Anne), 1962-
    A practical guide to assessing English language learners / Christine Coombe, Keith Folse,
Nancy Hubley.
        p. cm.
    Includes bibliographical references and index.
    ISBN-13: 978-0-472-03201-3 (pbk. : alk, paper)
    ISBN-10: 0-472-03201-1
    1. English language—Study and teaching—Foreign speakers—Evaluation. I. Folse,
Keith II. Hubley, Nancy III. Title.

PE1128.A2C6896 2007
378.1'662—dc22   2006053279

Preface

Travelers to a different country often buy a guidebook to understand the local culture, identify the main attractions, and learn a few helpful phrases to get around more easily. For many teachers of English language learners (ELLs), assessment is like visiting a foreign country. Assessment has its own culture, traditions, and special language. This guidebook is meant to help classroom teachers find their way more easily in the world of language assessment. The authors—experienced teachers and teacher-trainers—are your helpful tour guides. They will explain the important features of language assessment, point out essential phrases, and guide you on a journey of discovery as you learn how to make better use of assessment in your teaching.

Good assessment mirrors good teaching—they go hand in hand. Because there are such a great variety of English teaching settings, there are also a great variety of assessment techniques. Some teachers teach English as a second language (ESL) to adult learners in intensive English programs, in community colleges, or in adult education programs. Other teachers teach English as a foreign language (EFL) to children, adults, or both children and adult learners. Finally, some teachers teach regular content such as math or science to nonnative–speaking students in kindergarten, elementary, middle, or high schools (i.e., K–12) in English-speaking countries. This group can be referred to as ESOL (English to speakers of other languages), ELL, or even ESL learners. Regardless of the setting in which you teach, assessment should be a part of instruction from the very beginning of class planning.

In each chapter, you will encounter some ways two teachers (composites) deal with assessment in their classrooms. Ms. Wright, an experienced teacher well versed in assessment, models best practice while her less-experienced colleague, Mr. Knott, tries assessment concepts and techniques that are new to him. Through their experiences, you will:

- understand the cornerstones of all good assessment
- learn useful techniques for testing and alternative assessment
- become aware of issues in assessing reading, writing, listening, and speaking
- discover ways to help your students develop good test-taking strategies
- become familiar with the processes and procedures of assessment

Ms. Wright and Mr. Knott do not represent real individuals. They are composites of many teachers, all of whom have contributed to this book.

A final chapter focuses on the special needs of K–12 teachers in assessing English language learners in content areas, a major concern at a time of increased standardized testing.

The book starts with "Are You Testwise?" So why not start your journey with this pretest on page ix now?

Acknowledgments

This book resulted from our personal reflections as foreign/second language teachers and testers over many years in many different countries. It would not have been possible without the help and guidance of people we have encountered along the way.

We would like to thank our teaching colleagues at the UAE Higher Colleges of Technology and the University of Central Florida for their support and encouragement. We also recognize and thank the thousands of English language learners and workshop participants who have helped us hone these materials and, in the process, critiqued and improved our efforts.

All three of us want to thank our friends and family who have been so important in the completion of this book project. Christine is particularly grateful to Carl, Cindy, Marion, and Howard. Nancy appreciates the support of her college professor husband Woody and kindergarten teacher daughter Kristi with their practical concerns about classroom assessment.

Last, a special thanks to Kelly Sippell, editor at University of Michigan Press, for her guidance, encouragement, and thoughtful feedback.

Grateful acknowledgment is made to the following authors, publishers, and individuals for permission to reprint previously published materials.

Tom Cobb for the screen capture from the Vocabulary Profiler (p. 95).

Higher Colleges of Technology for the reproduction of marking scales for the assessment of debates and presentations.

Wayne Jones for table on Differences between Writing and Speaking (p. 114).

Dwight Lloyd for Sample Analytic Writing Criteria (p. 74) and for Sample Writing Prompt (p. 74), published in *The Fundamentals of Language Assessment: A Practical Guide for Teachers in the Gulf* by TESOL Arabia Testing, Assessment and Evaluation Special Interest Group.

The National Admissions and Placement Office (UAE) for the reproduction of the writing assessment scale from the Common Educational Proficiency Assessment (CEPA) (pp. 82–83).

Every effort has been made to contact the copyright holders for permission to reprint borrowed material. We regret any oversights that may have occurred and will rectify them in future printings of this book.

Contents

Are You Testwise?

Take this short quiz to discover how you'll benefit from reading this assessment book.

Read each situation and decide which is the <u>best</u> solution. Circle the letter of the best answer. You will find the answers on page xii. As you read, compare your responses with the chapter information.

1. It's the beginning of the semester, and you have a mixed-level class. You want to get an idea of the class's strengths and weaknesses before you plan your lessons. Which kind of test would give you the information you need? (You will find the answer to this question in the Introduction.)

   a. placement

   b. diagnostic

   c. proficiency

   d. aptitude

2. You've heard the phrase, "Test what you teach and how you teach it" many times. Which principle of good assessment does it exemplify? (You will find the answer to this question in the Introduction.)

   a. validity

   b. reliability

   c. washback

   d. practicality

3. Your college department team is planning the assessment strategy for the semester. You want to allocate sufficient time to each step of the assessment development process. Which step do most people tend to shortchange? (You will find the answer to this question in Chapter 1.)

   a. scheduling administration

   b. identification of outcomes

   c. establishing grading criteria

   d. analysis and reflection

4. You are writing a multiple choice exam for your students. Which is a potential threat to the reliability of your exam? (You will find the answer to this question in Chapter 2.)

   a. using three options as distractors

   b. keeping all common language in the stem

   c. providing an answer pattern (A B C D, A B C D, etc.)

   d. avoiding verbatim language from the text

5. Teachers often expand the True/False format to include a "not enough information" option. This has the advantage of reducing the guessing factor and requiring more cognitive processing of information. However, it's not appropriate for which language skill? (You will find the answer to this question in Chapter 2.)

   a. grammar

   b. listening

   c. reading

   d. vocabulary

6. You are about to assess student writing. What is the best strategy to ensure high reliability of your grading? (You will find the answer to this question in Chapter 4.)

   a. Require students to write a draft.

   b. Give students a very detailed prompt.

   c. Use multiple raters and a grading scale.

   d. Use free writing instead of guided writing.

7. Your class will soon sit for a high-stakes, standardized exam such as TOEFL®, PET, or IELTS™. What is the most helpful thing you can do to prepare the students? (You will find the answer to this question in Chapter 7.)

   a. Coach them in strategies such as time management.

   b. Give them additional mock examinations on a daily basis.

   c. Revise material that appeared on last year's exam.

   d. Stress the consequences of failing the examination.

8. Your last encounter with statistics was years ago at university. Now your principal has asked you to do some descriptive statistics on your students' grades. Which of these indicates the middle point in the distribution? (You will find the answer to this question in Chapter 9.)

   a. mean

   b. mode

   c. median

   d. standard deviation

9. Your colleagues are using multiple measures to assess students in a course. You want to find a type of alternative assessment that demonstrates what students can actually *do* as contrasted to what they *know* about the subject or skill. What's your **best** choice? (You will find the answer to this question in the Introduction.)

   a. an objective multiple choice question test

   b. a showcase portfolio

   c. reflective journals

   d. a project

10. Your institution has a number of campuses with expectations for common assessments. What is the best way to ensure that the students on each campus are assessed fairly? (You will find the answer to this question in Chapter 1.)

    a. Write to test specifications.

    b. Utilize student-designed tests.

    c. Recycle last year's tests.

    d. Use exams from the textbook.

This answer key for the pretest indicates the letter of the correct answer as well as the chapter and page(s) where you will find more information about the topic.

Question No.	Answer	Chapter	Page(s)
1	B	Introduction	xvi–xvii
2	A	Introduction	xxii
3	D	Chapter 1	12–13
4	C	Chapter 2	26, 30
5	B	Chapter 2	30–31
6	C	Chapter 4	80, 84, 86
7	A	Chapter 7	133–134, 136, 140
8	C	Chapter 9	161
9	D	Introduction	xx
10	A	Chapter 1	3

Introduction to Issues in Language Assessment and Terminology

In today's language classrooms, the term *assessment* usually evokes images of an end-of-course paper-and-pencil test designed to tell both teachers and students how much material the student doesn't know or hasn't yet mastered. However, assessment is much more than tests. Assessment includes a broad range of activities and tasks that teachers use to evaluate student progress and growth on a daily basis.

Consider a day in the life of Ms. Wright, a typical experienced ESL teacher in a large urban secondary school in Florida. In addition to her many administrative responsibilities, she engages in a wide range of assessment-related tasks on a daily basis. It is now May, two weeks before the end of the school year. Today, Ms. Wright did the following in her classroom:

- graded and analyzed yesterday's quiz on the irregular past tense
- decided on topics for tomorrow's review session
- administered a placement test to a new student to gauge the student's writing ability
- met with the principal to discuss the upcoming statewide exam
- checked her continuous assessment records to choose students to observe for speaking today
- improvised a review when it was clear that students were confused about yesterday's vocabulary lesson
- made arrangements to offer remediation to students who did poorly on last week's reading practice exam
- after reviewing the final exam that came with the textbook, decided to revise questions to suit class focus and coverage
- graded students' first drafts of a travel webquest using checklists distributed to students at the start of the project

Each of these tasks was based on a decision Ms. Wright made about her students or her class as a whole. Teachers assess their students in a number of ways and for a variety of purposes because they need to make decisions about their classrooms and their teaching. Some of these decisions are made on the spot, such as the improvised review. Others, like preparing the final exam, entail long-term planning.

Placing students in the right level of classroom instruction is an essential purpose of assessment. Normally, new students are given placement exams at the beginning of the school year, but some new students arrive throughout the year. By assigning a new student a writing task to gauge her writing ability, Ms. Wright tried to ensure that the student would benefit from instruction at the appropriate level for the remaining weeks of the school year.

Some of the decisions Ms. Wright made today had to do with **diagnosing student problems.** One of a teacher's main aims is to identify students' strengths and weaknesses with a view to carrying out revision or remedial activities. By making arrangements to offer remediation to students who did poorly on last week's reading exam, she was engaging in a form of **diagnostic assessment.**

Much of what teachers do today in language classrooms is to **find out about the language proficiency of their students.** In preparing her students to take the Florida Comprehensive Assessment Test (FCAT), Ms. Wright was determining whether her students have sufficient language proficiency to complete the exam effectively and meet national benchmarks.

Other activities were carried out with the aim of **evaluating academic performance.** In fact, a lot of teacher time is spent gathering information that will help teachers make decisions about their students' achievement regarding course goals and mastery of course content. Ms. Wright uses multiple measures such as quizzes, tests, projects, and continuous assessment to monitor her students' academic performance. To assign speaking grades to her students, she had to select four or five students per day for her continuous assessment records. These daily speaking scores will later be averaged together with her students' formal oral interview results for their final speaking grades.

Many of her classroom assessment activities concerned **instructional decision-making.** In deciding which material to present next or what to revise, Ms. Wright was making decisions about her language classroom. When she prepares her lesson plans, she consults the syllabus and the course objectives, but she also makes adjustments to suit the immediate needs of her students.

Some of the assessment activities that teachers participate in are for **accountability purposes.** Teachers must provide educational authorities with evidence that their intended learning outcomes have been achieved. Ms. Wright understands that her assessment decisions impact her students, their families, her school administration, and the community in which she works.

Evaluation, Assessment, and Testing

To help teachers make effective use of evaluation, assessment, and testing procedures in the foreign/second (F/SL) language classroom, it is necessary to clarify what these concepts are and explain how they differ from one another.

The term *evaluation* is all-inclusive and is the widest basis for collecting information in education. According to Brindley (1989), evaluation is "conceptualized as broader in scope, and concerned with the overall program" (p. 3). Evaluation involves looking at all factors that influence the learning process, i.e., syllabus objectives, course design, and materials (Harris & McCann, 1994). Evaluation goes beyond student achievement and language assessment to consider all aspects of teaching and learning and to look at how educational decisions can be informed by the results of alternative forms of assessment (Genessee, 2001).

Assessment is part of evaluation because it is concerned with the student and with what the student does (Brindley, 1989). *Assessment* refers to a variety of ways of collecting information on a learner's language ability or achievement. Although *testing* and *assessment* are often used interchangeably, *assessment* is an umbrella term for all types of measures used to evaluate student progress. *Tests* are a subcategory of assessment. A *test* is a formal, systematic (usually paper-and-pencil) procedure used to gather information about students' behavior.

In summary, *evaluation* includes the whole course or program, and information is collected from many sources, including the learner. While *assessment* is related to the learner and his or her achievements, *testing* is part of assessment, and it measures learner achievement.

Categorizing Assessment Tasks

Different types of tests are administered for different purposes and used at different stages of the course to gather information about students. You as a language teacher have the responsibility of deciding on the best option for your particular group of students in your particular teaching context. It is useful to categorize assessments by type, purpose, or place within the teaching/learning process or timing.

Types of Tests

The most common use of language tests is to identify strengths and weaknesses in students' abilities. For example, through testing we might discover that a student has excellent oral language abilities but a relatively low level of reading comprehension. Information gleaned from tests also assists us in deciding who should be allowed to participate in a particular course or program area. Another common use of tests is to provide information about the effectiveness of programs of instruction.

Placement Tests

Placement tests assess students' level of language ability so they can be placed in an appropriate course or class. This type of test indicates the level at which a student will learn most effectively. The primary aim is to create groups of learners that are homogeneous in level. In designing a placement test, the test developer may base the test content either on a theory of general language proficiency or on learning objectives of the curriculum. Institutions may choose to use a well-established proficiency test such as the TOEFL®, IELTS™, or MELAB exam and link it to curricular benchmarks. Alternatively, some placement tests are based on aspects of the syllabus taught at the institution concerned (Alderson, Clapham, & Wall, 1995).

At some institutions, students are placed according to their overall rank in the test results combined from all skills. At other schools and colleges, students are placed according to their level in each skill area. Additionally, placement test scores are used to determine if a student needs further instruction in the language or could matriculate directly into an academic program without taking preparatory language courses.

Aptitude Tests

An *aptitude test* measures capacity or general ability to learn a foreign or second language. Although not commonly used these days, two examples deserve mention: the Modern Language Aptitude Test (MLAT) developed by Carroll and Sapon in 1958 and the Pimsleur Language Aptitude Battery (PLAB) developed by Pimsleur in 1966 (Brown, H.D., 2004). These are used primarily in deciding to sponsor a person for special training based on language aptitude.

Diagnostic Tests

Diagnostic tests identify language areas in which a student needs further help. Harris and McCann (1994) point out that where "other types of tests are based on success, diagnostic tests are based on failure" (p. 29). The information gained from diagnostic tests is crucial for further course activities and providing students with remediation. Because diagnostic tests are difficult to write, placement tests often serve a dual function of both placement and diagnosis (Harris & McCann, 1994; Davies et al., 1999).

Progress Tests

Progress tests measure the progress that students are making toward defined course or program goals. They are administered at various stages throughout a language course to determine what students have learned, usually after certain segments of instruction have been completed. Progress tests are generally teacher produced and narrower in focus than achievement tests because they cover less material and assess fewer objectives.

Achievement Tests

Achievement tests are similar to progress tests in that they determine what a student has learned with regard to stated course outcomes. They are usually administered at mid- and end-point of the semester or academic year. The content of achievement tests is generally based on the specific course content or on the course objectives. Achievement tests are often cumulative, covering material drawn from an entire course or semester.

Proficiency Tests

Proficiency tests, on the other hand, are not based on a particular curriculum or language program. They assess the overall language ability of students at varying levels. They may also tell us how capable a person is in a particular language skill area (e.g., reading). In other words, proficiency tests describe what students are capable of doing in a language.

Proficiency tests are typically developed by external bodies such as examination boards like Educational Testing Services (ETS), the College Board, or Cambridge ESOL. Some proficiency tests have been standardized for international use, such as the TOEFL®, which measures the English language proficiency of foreign college students who wish to study in North American universities or the IELTS™, which is intended for those who wish to study in the United Kingdom or Australia (Davies et al., 1999). Increasingly, North American universities are accepting IELTS™ as a measure of English language proficiency.

Additional Ways of Labeling Tests

Objective versus Subjective Tests

Sometimes tests are distinguished by the manner in which they are scored. An *objective test* is scored by comparing a student's responses with an established set of acceptable/correct responses on an answer key. With objectively scored tests, the scorer does not require particular knowledge or training in the examined area. In contrast, a *subjective test,* such as writing an essay, requires scoring by opinion or personal judgment so the human element is very important.

Testing formats associated with objective tests are multiple choice questions (MCQs), True/False/Not Given (T/F/Ns), and matching. Objectively scored tests are ideal for computer scanning. Examples of subjectively scored tests are essay tests, interviews, or comprehension questions. Even experienced scorers or markers need moderated training sessions to ensure inter-rater reliability.

Criterion-Referenced versus Norm-Referenced or Standardized Tests

Criterion-referenced tests (CRTs) are usually developed to measure mastery of well-defined instructional objectives specific to a particular course or program. Their purpose is to measure how much learning has occurred. Student performance is compared only to the amount or percentage of material learned (Brown, J.D., 2005).

True CRTs are devised before instruction is designed so that the test will match the teaching objectives. This lessens the possibility that teachers will "teach to the test." The criterion or cut-off score is set in advance. Student achievement is measured with respect to the degree of learning or mastery of the pre-specified content. A primary concern of a CRT is that it be sensitive to different ability levels.

Norm-referenced tests (NRT) or standardized tests differ from criterion-referenced tests in a number of ways. NRTs are designed to measure global language abilities. Students' scores are interpreted relative to all other students who take the exam. The purpose of an NRT is to spread students out along a continuum of scores so that those with low abilities in a certain skill are at one end of the normal distribution and those with high scores are at the other end, with the majority of the students falling between the extremes (Brown, J.D., 2005, p. 2).

By definition, an NRT must have been previously administered to a large sample of people from the target population. Acceptable standards of achievement are determined after the test has been developed and administered. Test results are interpreted with reference to the performance of a given group or norm. The *norm* is typically a large group of students who are similar to the individuals for whom the test is designed.

Summative versus Formative

Tests or tasks administered at the end of the course to determine if students have achieved the objectives set out in the curriculum are called *summative assessments.* They are often used to decide which students move on to a higher level (Harris & McCann, 1994). *Formative assessments,* however, are carried out with the aim of using the results to improve instruction, so they are given during a course and feedback is provided to students.

High-Stakes versus Low-Stakes Tests

High-stakes tests are those in which the results are likely to have a major impact on the lives of large numbers of individuals or on large programs. For example, the TOEFL® is high stakes in that admission to a university program is often contingent on receiving a sufficient language proficiency score.

Low-stakes tests are those in which the results have a relatively minor impact on the lives of the individual or on small programs. In-class progress tests or short quizzes are examples of low-stakes tests.

Traditional versus Alternative Assessment

One useful way of understanding alternative assessment is to contrast it with traditional testing. *Alternative assessment* asks students to show what they can do; students are evaluated on what they integrate and produce rather than on what they are able to recall and reproduce (Huerta-Macias, 1995). Competency-based assessment demonstrates what students can actually *do* with English. Alternative assessment differs from traditional testing in that it:

- does not intrude on regular classroom activities
- reflects the curriculum actually being implemented in the classroom
- provides information on the strengths and weaknesses of each individual student
- provides multiple indices that can be used to gauge student progress
- is more multiculturally sensitive and free of the linguistic and cultural biases found in traditional testing (Huerta-Macias, 1995).

Types of Alternative Assessment

Several types of alternative assessment can be used with great success in today's language classrooms:

- Self-assessment
- Portfolio assessment
- Student-designed tests
- Learner-centered assessment
- Projects
- Presentations

Specific types of alternative assessment will be discussed in the skills chapters.

This chart summarizes common types of language assessment.

Table 1: Common Types of Language Assessment	
Informal	Formal
Classroom, "low-stakes"	Standardized, "high-stakes"
Criterion-referenced	Norm-referenced
Achievement	Proficiency
Direct	Indirect
Subjective	Objective
Formative	Summative
Alternative, authentic	Traditional tests

Because language performance depends heavily on the purpose for language use and the context in which it is used, it makes sense to provide students with assessment opportunities that reflect these practices. *Our assessment practices must reflect the importance of using language both in and out of the language classroom.*

It is also important to note that most testers today recommend that teachers use *multiple measures assessment*. Multiple measures assessment comes from the belief that no single measure of language assessment is enough to tell us all we need to know about our students' language abilities. That is, we must employ a mixture of all the assessment types previously mentioned to obtain an accurate reading of our students' progress and level of language proficiency.

Test Purpose

One of the most important first tasks of any test writer is to determine the purpose of the test. Defining the purpose aids in selection of the right type of test. This table shows the purpose of many of the common test types.

Table 2: Common Test Types	
Test Type	**Main Purpose**
Placement tests	Place students at appropriate level of instruction within program
Diagnostic tests	Identify students' strengths and weaknesses for remediation
Progress tests or in-course tasks	Provide information about mastery or difficulty with course materials
Achievement tests	Provide information about students' attainment of course outcomes at end of course or within the program
Standardized tests	Provide measure of students' proficiency using international benchmarks

Timing of the Test

Tests are commonly categorized by the point in the instructional period at which they occur. Aptitude, admissions, and general proficiency tests often take place before or outside of the program; placement and diagnostic tests often occur at the start of a program. Progress and achievement tests take place during the course of instruction and promotion, while mastery or certification tests occur at the end of a course of study or program.

The Cornerstones of Testing

Language testing at any level is a highly complex undertaking that must be based on theory as well as practice. Although this book focuses on practical aspects of classroom testing, an understanding of the basic principles of larger-scale testing is essential. The nine guiding principles that govern good test design, development, and analysis are *usefulness, validity, reliability, practicality, washback, authenticity, transparency, and security.* Repeated references to these cornerstones of language testing will be made throughout this book.

Usefulness

For Bachman and Palmer (1996), the most important consideration in designing and developing a language test is the use for which it is intended: "Test usefulness provides a kind of metric by which we can evaluate not only the tests that we develop and use, but also all aspects of test development and use" (p. 17). Thus, *usefulness* is the most important quality or cornerstone of testing. Bachman and Palmer's model of test usefulness requires that any language test must be developed with a specific purpose, a particular group of test-takers, and a specific language use in mind.

Validity

The term *validity* refers to the extent to which a test measures what it purports to measure. In other words, *test what you teach and how you teach it!* Types of validity include content, construct, and face validity. For classroom teachers, *content validity* means that the test assesses the course content and outcomes using formats familiar to the students. *Construct validity* refers to the "fit" between the underlying theories and methodology of language learning and the type of assessment. For example, a communicative language learning approach must be matched by communicative language testing. *Face validity* means that the test looks as though it measures what it is supposed to measure. This is an important factor for both students and administrators. Moreover, a professional-looking exam has more credibility with students and administrators than a sloppy one.

It is important to be clear about what we want to assess and then be certain that we are assessing that material and not something else. Making sure that clear assessment objectives are met is of primary importance in achieving test validity. The best way to ensure validity is to produce tests to specifications. See Chapter 1 regarding the use of specifications.

Reliability

Reliability refers to the consistency of test scores, which simply means that a test would offer similar results if it were given at another time. For example, if the same test were to be administered to the same group of students at two different times in two different settings, it should not make any difference to the test-taker whether he or she takes the test on one occasion and in one setting or the other. Similarly, if we develop two forms of a test that are intended to be used interchangeably, it should not make any difference to the test-taker which form or version of the test he or she takes. The student should obtain approximately the same score on either form or version of the test. Versions of exams that are not equivalent can be a threat to reliability, the use of specifications is strongly recommended; developing all versions of a test according to specifications can ensure equivalency across the versions.

Three important factors affect test reliability. Test factors such as the formats and content of the questions and the time given for students to take the exam must be consistent. For example, testing research shows that longer exams produce more reliable results than brief quizzes (Bachman, 1990, p. 220). In general, the more items on a test, the more reliable it is considered to be because teachers have more samples of students' language ability. Administrative factors are also important for reliability. These include the classroom setting (lighting, seating arrangements, acoustics, lack of intrusive noise, etc.) and how the teacher manages the administration of the exam. Affective factors in the response of individual students can also affect reliability, as can fatigue, personality type, and learning style. Test anxiety can be allayed by coaching students in good test-taking strategies.

A fundamental concern in the development and use of language tests is to identify potential sources of error in a given measure of language ability and to minimize the effect of these factors on test reliability. Henning (1987) describes these threats to test reliability.

- **Fluctuations in the Learner.** A variety of changes may take place within the learner that may change a learner's true score from test to test. Examples of this type of change might be additional learning or forgetting. Influences such as fatigue, sickness, emotional problems, and practice effect may cause the learner's score to deviate from the score that reflects his or her actual ability. Practice effect means that a student's score could improve because he or she has taken the test so many times that the content is familiar.

- **Fluctuations in Scoring.** Subjectivity in scoring or mechanical errors in the scoring process may introduce error into scores and affect the reliability of the test's results. These kinds of errors usually occur within (intra-rater) or between (inter-rater) the raters themselves.
- **Fluctuations in Test Administration.** Inconsistent administrative procedures and testing conditions will reduce test reliability. This problem is most common in institutions where different groups of students are tested in different locations on different days.

Reliability is an essential quality of test scores because unless test scores are relatively consistent, they cannot provide us with information about the abilities we want to measure. A common theme in the assessment literature is the idea that reliability and validity are closely interlocked. While reliability focuses on the empirical aspects of the measurement process, validity focuses on the theoretical aspects and interweaves these concepts with the empirical ones (Davies et al., 1999, p. 169). For this reason it is easier to assess reliability than validity.

Practicality

Another important feature of a good test is practicality. Classroom teachers know all too well the importance of familiar practical issues, but they need to think of how practical matters relate to testing. For example, a good classroom test should be "teacher friendly." A teacher should be able to develop, administer, and mark it within the available time and with available resources. Classroom tests are only valuable to students when they are returned promptly and when the feedback from assessment is understood by the student. In this way, students can benefit from the test-taking process. Practical issues include the cost of test development and maintenance, adequate time (for development and test length), resources (everything from computer access, copying facilities, and AV equipment to storage space), ease of marking, availability of suitable/trained graders, and administrative logistics. For example, teachers know that ideally it would be good to test speaking one-on-one for up to ten minutes per student. However, for a class of 25 students, this could take four hours. In addition, what would the teachers do with the other 24 students during the testing?

Washback

Washback refers to the effect of testing on teaching and learning. Washback is generally said to be positive or negative. Unfortunately, students and teachers tend to think of the negative effects of testing such as "test-driven" curricula and only studying and learning "what they need to know for the test." In contrast, positive washback, or what we prefer to call *guided washback,* benefits teachers, students, and administrators because it assumes that testing and curriculum design are both based on clear course outcomes that are known to both students and teachers/testers. If students perceive that tests are markers of their progress toward achieving these outcomes, they have a sense of accomplishment.

Authenticity

Language learners are motivated to perform when they are faced with tasks that reflect real-world situations and contexts. Good testing or assessment strives to use formats and tasks that mirror the types of situations in which students would authentically use the target language. Whenever possible, teachers should attempt to use authentic materials in testing language skills. For K–12 teachers of content courses, the use of authentic materials at the appropriate language level provides additional exposure to concepts and vocabulary as students will encounter them in real-life situations.

Transparency

Transparency refers to the availability of clear, accurate information to students about testing. Such information should include outcomes to be evaluated, formats used, weighting of items and sections, time allowed to complete the test, and grading criteria. Transparency dispels the myths and mysteries surrounding testing and the sometimes seemingly adversarial relationship between learning and assessment. Transparency makes students part of the testing process.

Security

Most teachers feel that security is an issue only in large-scale, high-stakes testing. However, security is part of both reliability and validity for all tests. If a teacher invests time and energy in developing good tests that accurately reflect the course outcomes, then it is desirable to be able to recycle the test materials. Recycling is especially important if analyses show that the items, distractors, and test sections are valid and discriminating. In some parts of the world, cultural attitudes toward "collaborative test-taking" are a threat to test security and thus to reliability and validity. As a result, there is a trade-off between letting tests into the public domain and giving students adequate information about tests.

Ten Things to Remember

1. **Test <u>what</u> has been taught and <u>how</u> it has been taught.**
   This is the basic concept of content validity. In achievement testing, it is important to only test students on what has been covered in class and to do this through formats and techniques they are familiar with.

2. **Set tasks in context whenever possible.**
   This is the basic concept of authenticity. Authenticity is just as important in language testing as it is in language teaching. Whenever possible, develop assessment tasks that mirror purposeful real-life situations.

3. **Choose formats that are authentic for tasks and skills.**
   Although challenging at times, it is better to select formats and techniques that are purposeful and relevant to real-life contexts.

4. **Specify the material to be tested.**
   This is the basic concept of transparency. It is crucial that students have information about how they will be assessed and have access to the criteria on which they will be assessed. This transparency will lower students' test anxiety.

5. **Acquaint students with techniques and formats prior to testing.**
   Students should never be exposed to a new format or technique in a testing situation. Doing so could affect the reliability of your test/assessment. Don't avoid new formats; just introduce them to your classes in a low-stress environment outside the testing situation.

6. **Administer the test in uniform, non-distracting conditions.**
   Another threat to the reliability of your test is the way in which you administer the assessment. Make sure your testing conditions and procedures are consistent among different groups of students.

7. **Provide timely feedback.**
   Feedback is of no value if it arrives in the students' hands too late to do anything with it. Provide feedback to students in a timely manner. Give easily scored objective tests back during the next class. Aim to return subjective tests that involve more grading within three class periods.

8. **Reflect on the exam without delay.**
   Often teachers are too tired after marking the exam to do anything else. Don't shortchange the last step—that of reflection. Remember, all stakeholders in the exam process (that includes you, the teacher) must benefit from the exam.

9. **Make changes based on analyses and feedback from colleagues and students.**
   An important part of the reflection phase is the opportunity to revise the exam when it is still fresh in your mind. This important step will save you time later in the process.

10. **Employ multiple measures assessment in your classes.**
    Use a variety of types of assessment to determine the language abilities of your students. No one type of assessment can give you all the information you need to accurately assess your students.

Extension Activity

Cornerstones Case Study

Read this case study about Mr. Knott, a colleague of Ms. Wright's, and try to spot the cornerstones violations. What could be done to solve these problems?

Background Information

Mr. Knott is a high school ESL and Spanish teacher. His current teaching load is two ESL classes. His students come from many language backgrounds and cultures. In his classes, he uses an integrated-skills textbook that espouses a communicative methodology.

His Test

Mr. Knott firmly believes in the KISS philosophy of "keeping it short and simple." Most recently he has covered modal verbs in his classes. He decides to give his students only one question to test their knowledge about modal verbs: "Write a 300-word essay on the meanings of modal verbs and their stylistic uses. Give examples and be specific." Because he was short of time, he distributed a handwritten prompt on unlined paper. Incidentally, he gave this same test last year.

Information Given to Students

To keep students on their toes and to increase attendance, he told them that the test could occur anytime during the week. Of his two classes, Mr. Knott has a preference for his morning class because they are much more well behaved and hard working so he hinted during the class that modal verbs might be the focus of the test. His afternoon class received no information on the topic of the test.

Test Administration Procedures

Mr. Knott administered his test to his afternoon class on Monday and to his morning class on Thursday. Always wanting to practice his Spanish, he clarified the directions for his Spanish-speaking students in Spanish. During the Monday administration, his test was interrupted by a fire drill. Since this was the first time a fire drill had happened, he did not have any back-up plan for collecting test papers. Consequently, some students took their papers with them. In the confusion, several test papers were mislaid.

Grading Procedures

Mr. Knott didn't tell his students when to expect their results. Due to his busy schedule, he graded tests over several days during the next week. Students finally got their tests back ten days later. Because the test grades were extremely low, Mr. Knott added ten points to everyone's paper to achieve a good curve.

Post-Exam Follow-Up Procedures

Mr. Knott entered grades in his grade book but didn't annotate or analyze them. Although Mr. Knott announced in class that the exam was worth 15 percent of the students' grade, he downgraded it to five percent. Next year he plans to recycle the same test but will require students to write 400 words.

What's wrong with Mr. Knott's testing procedures? Your chart should look something like this.

Cornerstone Violation	Mr. Knott's Problem	Possible Solution
	Construct validity violation: • He espouses a communicative language teaching philosophy but gives a test that is not communicative.	
	Authenticity violation: • Writing about verb functions is not an authentic use of language.	Mr. Knott should have chosen tasks that required students to use modal verbs in real-life situations.
	Practicality violation: • He was short of time and distributed a handwritten test.	Mr. Knott probably waited until the last minute and threw something together in panic mode.
	Face validity violation: • He distributed a hand-written prompt on unlined paper.	Tests must have a professional look.
	Security violation: • He gave the same test last year, and it's probably in the public domain.	If a test was administered verbatim the previous year, there is a strong probability that students already have access to it. Teachers should make every effort to produce parallel forms of tests that are secure.

Cornerstone Violation	Mr. Knott's Problem	Possible Solution
Information Given to Students	**Transparency violation:** • He preferred one class over another (potential bias) and gave them more information about the test.	Mr. Knott needs to provide the same type and amount of information to all students.
Test Administration Procedures	**Security violation:** • He administered the same test to both classes three days apart. • Some students took their papers outside during the fire drill. • Some students lost their papers. **Reliability/transparency violation:** • His Spanish-speaking students got directions in Spanish.	When administering the same test to different classes, an effort should be made to administer the tests close together so as to prevent test leaks. Mr. Knott should have disallowed this test due to security breaches. The same type and amount of information should be given to all students.
Grading Procedures	**Transparency violation:** • Students didn't know when to expect their results. **Reliability violation:** • He graded test papers over the course of a week (i.e., there was potential for intra-rater reliability problems). **Washback violation:** • Students got their papers back ten days later so there was no chance for remediation.	Teachers should return test papers to students no longer than three class periods after the test was administered. It would have been better to grade all the papers in a shorter period of time to ensure a similar internal standard of marking. As students were already into the next set of objectives, they had no opportunity to practice material they did poorly on. Teachers should always return papers in a timely manner and review topics that proved problematic for students.

Cornerstone Violation	Mr. Knott's Problem	Possible Solution
Post-Exam Follow-Up Procedures	**Security violation:** • He plans to recycle the test yet again.	Only good tests should be recycled. Mr. Knott's students didn't do so well on this test, and he had to curve the grades. This should tell Mr. Knott that the test needs to be retired or seriously revised.

The Process of Developing Assessment

We have seen that assessment covers a range of activities from everyday observation of students' performance in class to large-scale standardized exams. Some teachers will be involved in a full range of assessment activities, while others will mainly be responsible for producing informal assessments for their own classes. However, at one time or another, almost all teachers are consumers of tests prepared by other people, so regardless of their personal involvement in actually developing assessment, teachers can benefit from understanding the processes involved. This chapter provides a guide to the assessment development process.

Assessment includes the phases of planning, development, administration, analysis, feedback, and reflection. Depending on teaching load and other professional responsibilities, a teacher can be working in several different phases at any one time. Let's look at how this applies in the case of Ms. Wright, an assessment leader in her high school.

If we were to visit Ms. Wright in early November, halfway through the fall semester, we would learn that she had already taken these steps toward assessment of her students:

- started planning in August by doing an inventory of her Grade 12 course, ensuring that outcomes closely matched assessment specifications
- met with her colleagues to develop a schedule of different types of assessment spaced throughout the academic year
- ensured that all stakeholders (students, parents, colleagues, administration) had information about when assessments

occur, what they entail, and how much each assessment is worth

- administered and analyzed diagnostic exams to her classes in September and adjusted her instruction to the needs of her students
- revisited previous midterm and final exams to review results and select items for recycling based on item analysis conducted after the last test administration
- asked colleagues to prepare new test items well in advance of exams to allow time for editing
- organized workshops on speaking and writing to ensure inter-rater reliability
- blocked out time to conduct a preliminary analysis soon after the midterm exam
- scheduled a meeting with administrators to discuss midterm results

Figure 1: Assessment in the Teaching/Learning Cycle

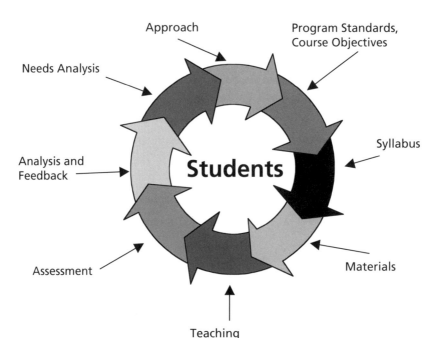

Assessment is an integral part of the entire curriculum cycle, not something tacked on as an afterthought to teaching. Therefore, decisions about how to assess students must be considered from the very beginning of curriculum design or course planning. Once a needs analysis has established the goals and approach for an English program, *standards* are developed that define the overall aims for a particular level of instruction. These standards are then converted to more specific *course objectives* or *outcomes* that state what a student can be expected to achieve or accomplish in a particular course. It is important that the outcomes are worded in terms of actual student performance because they form the basis for the development of assessment *specifications,* which are the planning documents or "recipes" for particular assessments such as tests and projects.

An outcome such as "Students will study present tenses" is too vague to be transformed into a test specification. If the outcomes are restated as "Students will use the simple present to describe facts, routines, and states of being" and "Students will use the present continuous (progressive) to describe an activity currently in progress," then it is much easier to create specifications that check that a student understands which tense to use in a particular circumstance. You can then choose whether to test these tenses separately or together, select formats that suit your purpose, and decide whether to have students produce answers or simply identify correct responses.

Looking again at how assessment fits in with the rest of the curriculum, we note the importance of analysis and feedback. Administrators are always eager to get results such as grades from assessments, but it is equally important to make time for analysis. Thorough analysis can identify constructive changes for other components of the program such as syllabus sequencing, textbook choice, or teaching strategies. Analysis is the basis for helpful feedback to students, teachers, and administrators. Assessment coupled with analysis can improve instruction; assessment alone cannot.

The Assessment Process

The six major steps in the assessment process are: (1) planning, (2) development, (3) administration, (4) analysis, (5) feedback, and (6) reflection. In turn, each step consists of a number of component steps. This flow chart will help you follow the first stages of the process.

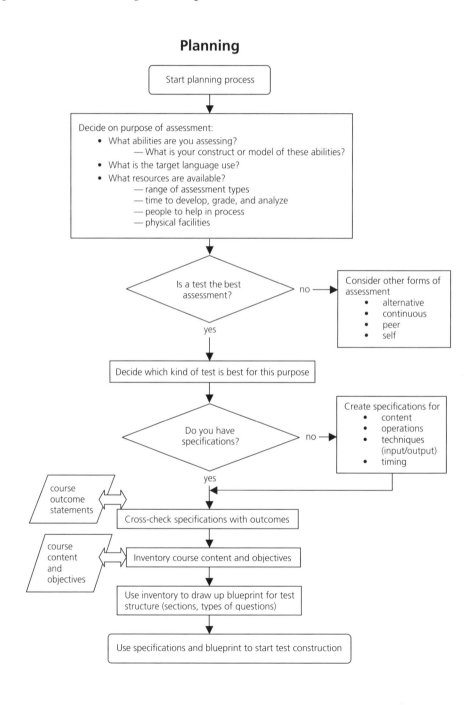

Planning

Start planning process

Decide on purpose of assessment:
- What abilities are you assessing?
  — What is your construct or model of these abilities?
- What is the target language use?
- What resources are available?
  — range of assessment types
  — time to develop, grade, and analyze
  — people to help in process
  — physical facilities

Is a test the best assessment?

no → Consider other forms of assessment
- alternative
- continuous
- peer
- self

yes

Decide which kind of test is best for this purpose

Do you have specifications?

no → Create specifications for
- content
- operations
- techniques (input/output)
- timing

yes

course outcome statements

Cross-check specifications with outcomes

course content and objectives

Inventory course content and objectives

Use inventory to draw up blueprint for test structure (sections, types of questions)

Use specifications and blueprint to start test construction

Planning

Choosing Assessment for Your Needs

Several steps are important in planning for assessment. First, you must consider *why* you are assessing and choose a type of assessment that fits your needs. What is the purpose of this assessment, and what kind of information do you need to get from it? Is a test the best means of assessment at this point, or would some form of alternative assessment do the job better? What abilities do you want to measure, and what kind of mental model, or *construct,* do you have of these abilities? For example, do you consider listening to be predominantly a receptive skill, or is listening so closely paired with speaking in interactive situations that you must assess the two skills together? For your purposes at this time, is it important to assess a skill directly by having students produce writing or is it sufficient to indirectly test some aspects of their writing?

Bachman and Palmer (1996) emphasize the importance of "target language use (TLU) domain," which they define as "tasks that the test taker is likely to encounter outside of the test itself, and to which we want our inferences about language ability to generalize" (p. 44). They further distinguish "real-life domains" that resemble communication situations students will encounter in daily life from "language instruction domains" featured in teaching and learning situations. For a student planning to work in an office, learning how to take messages would be an example of the former, while note-taking during lectures exemplifies the latter. In both cases, teachers need to take the target language use into account in the initial stages of their assessment planning and choose assessment tasks that reflect TLU domains in realistic or authentic ways.

If you are assessing progress or achievement in a particular part of the syllabus, you need to "map" the content and main objectives of this section of the course. Remember that you cannot assess everything, so you have to make choices about *what* to assess. Some teachers find it helpful to visualize assessment as an album of student progress that contains photographs and mementos of a wide range of work. Just as a snapshot captures a single image, a test or quiz shows a student's performance at one point in time. The mementos are samples of other kinds of student performance such as journal entries, reports, or graphics used in a presentation. All of these together offer a broader picture of the student's linguistic ability. Thus, in deciding what to assess, you also have to decide the best means of assessment for those objectives.

As you map the material to be assessed, there are several other factors to be considered: What weighting do you assign to the objectives? Are they equally important, or are some more fundamental to the course as a whole? Is this assessment focused on recent material, or does it comprehensively include material from earlier in the course? Which skills do you plan to assess, and will you test them separately or integrate them? Sometimes time and resources constrain the skills that you can practically assess, but it is important to avoid the trap of choosing items or tasks simply because they are easy to create or grade. As always, testing should reflect teaching and the amount of time spent on something in the classroom.

Mapping out the course content and objectives is not the only kind of inventory. At this stage of assessment planning, you must also take stock of other kinds of resources that may determine your choices. What realistic assessment options do you have in your teaching situation? If all your colleagues use tests and quizzes, can you opt for portfolios and interviews? How much time do you have to design, develop, administer, grade, and analyze assessment? Do you have the physical facilities to support your choice? For example, if you decide to have students videotape each other's presentations, is this feasible? How much lead time do you need to print and collate paper-and-pencil exams? Computer-based testing may sound great, but do you have the appropriate software, hardware, and technical support? These are a simple handful of important aspects to consider in determining what your assessment will look like.

Autonomy is another factor in planning assessment. Typically, assessment is coordinated with other colleagues in a department, with teachers using common tests for midterm and final examinations as well as agreeing on alternative assessment tasks for a course. This arrangement may mean that you have autonomy for some kinds of classroom assessment but are expected to contribute to the design and grading of assessments done on a larger scale. In other cases, notably at the college level, teachers have more autonomy in planning which kinds of assessment to use for their own classes. It can be a real advantage to work collaboratively as part of an assessment team because each person benefits from the input and constructive suggestions of other people. If you do work by yourself, find colleagues who teach similar courses and are willing to work with you and give feedback. In either a centralized or autonomous situation, it is useful to develop specifications to ensure continuity and reliability from one instructor or semester to another.

Specifications

A *specification* is a detailed description of exactly *what* is being assessed and *how* it is being done. In large institutions and for standardized public examinations, specifications become official documents that clearly state all the components and criteria for assessment. However, for the average classroom teacher, much simpler specifications provide an opportunity to clarify your assessment decisions. When several colleagues contribute individual items or sections to a "home-grown" assessment, specifications provide a common set of criteria for development and evaluation. By agreeing to use a common "recipe" or "formula," all contributors share a clear idea of expectations. An assessment instrument built on specifications is coherent and cohesive. If a test has multiple versions, specifications provide a kind of "quality control" so that the versions are truly comparable and thus reliable. Moreover, the use of specifications contributes to transparency and accountability because the underlying rationale is made very explicit.

Specifications can be simple or complex, depending on the context for assessment. As a rule, the more formal and higher-stakes the assessment, the more detailed specifications need to be to ensure validity and reliability. There are several excellent language testing books that provide detailed discussions of specification development. For example, Alderson, Clapham, and Wall's (1995) chapter on test specifications concludes with a useful checklist of 21 components (p. 38), while Davidson and Lynch's (2002) entire book is devoted to writing and using language test specifications. Davidson and Lynch define the essential components of specifications. For classroom purposes, far simpler specifications might include:

- a general description of the assessment
- a list of skills to be tested and operations students should be able to do
- the techniques for assessing those skills
  - —the formats and tasks to be used
  - —the types of prompts given for each task
  - —the expected type of response for each task
  - —the timing for the task
- the expected level of performance and grading criteria

Examples of specifications are provided in each of the skills chapters (i.e., Chapters 3–6).

In discussing item types and tasks, H. D. Brown (2004) makes a useful distinction between elicitation and response modes. Elicitation modes refer to ways in which responses are prompted, whereas response modes refer to ways a student can respond to a question. Students listen to an oral prompt or read a written prompt then respond through speaking or writing (p. 51). For example, students could listen to a dialogue as an oral prompt and then write short answers in response. Within each mode, there are many different options for formats. It is important to avoid skill contamination by requiring too much prompt reading for a listening task or giving a long listening prompt for a writing task because that tests memory and not listening skills. The chart that follows makes these combinations of prompts and responses clearer.

Prompt	Oral (listening)	Oral (listening)	Written (reading)	Written (reading)
Response	Speaking	Writing	Speaking	Writing

Some of the most common item formats and assessment tasks are detailed in Chapter 2. Sometimes the range of options seems daunting, especially to teachers without much experience in writing exams. Hughes (2003) makes the practical suggestion of using professionally designed exams as sources for inspiration (p. 59). Using published materials as models for writing your own versions is quite different from the practice of adapting or copying exams that were developed for other circumstances. Teachers who have to produce many assessments often keep a file of interesting formats or ideas that they modify to suit their own assessment situations. Make note of topics that appear in textbooks or on standardized exams and collect potential assessment material related to these topics.

A close inspection of the formats used in standardized examinations can be beneficial for both students and teachers. As a consequence of the No Child Left Behind policy, American students now take more high-stakes standardized exams than in the recent past. The results are used to judge teacher and school performance as well as that of students. An analysis of how the exams are organized and how the items are built often clarifies the intent of the test designers and their priorities. Professional testing organizations develop their assessments based on specifications. If you can deduce what these specifications are, you have a better understanding of how high-stakes exams are constructed, and you can also incorporate some of their features in your own assessments. This knowledge will benefit your students because they will be familiar with the operations and types of tasks that they will encounter later. In their guide to writing specifications, Davidson and Lynch

(2002) call this analysis of underlying specifications "reverse engineering" (pp. 41–44).

After you have your specifications well in hand, cross-check them with the course outcome statements to make sure the things you have decided to assess align with the major course objectives. Assessment design is an iterative or looping process in which you often return to your starting point, all in the interest of ensuring continuity between teaching and assessment.

Previous exams written to the same specifications and thoroughly analyzed after previous administrations are a tried-and-true source for exam items. If the exam was administered under secure conditions and kept secure, it is possible to recycle some items. The most logical candidates for recycling in a short period of time are discrete grammar or vocabulary items. Items that have fared well in item analysis can be slightly modified and used again. Exam sections that depend on long reading texts or listening passages are best kept secure for several years before recycling.

Although specifications usually refer to the form and content of tests or examinations (Davidson & Lynch, 2002), they are just as useful for other forms of assessment. In a multiple measures assessment plan, it is advisable to have specifications for any assessments that will be used by more than one teacher to ensure reliability between classes. For example, if 12 teachers have students working on projects, the expectations for what each project will include and how it will be graded should be clear to everyone involved.

Constructing the Assessment

At this point, you have used your specifications for the overall design of the assessment and to write sections and individual items. If you worked as part of a team, your colleagues have carefully examined items you wrote as you have scrutinized theirs. Despite good intentions, all item writers produce some items that need to be edited or even rejected. A question that is very clear to the writer can be interpreted in a very different way by a fresh reader. For example, students sometimes produce unanticipated responses for short answers or gap-fill items or have an entirely different interpretation of the prompt or task. It is far better to catch ambiguities and misunderstandings at the test construction stage than later when the test is administered!

The next step is to prepare an answer key and scoring system for writing and speaking. Specific suggestions for grading will be given in Chapters 3, 4, 5, and 6 that focus on skills. The answer key should give any alternative answers for open-ended questions and specify the degree of accuracy expected in spelling, for example. The length or duration of production should also be made clear (e.g., *write 250 words, speak for two minutes,* etc.). Decide on cut-off points or acceptable levels of mastery but be prepared to adjust them later. Design the answer key so that it is clear and ready to use.

Once the assessment is assembled, it is advisable to pilot it. Ideally, the test should be trialed with a group that is very similar to those who will use it, perhaps at another school or location. Don't tell students that they are taking the exam as a trial because that will affect their scores. If a trial with similar students is not possible, have colleagues take the test, adjusting the timing to allow for their level of competency.

Next, compare the answer key and scoring system with the results from the trial. Were there any unexpected answers that now must be considered? Are some items unclear or ambiguous? Are there any typographical errors or other physical/layout problems? Make any adjustments and finalize plans to reproduce the exam. Check that all necessary resources are available or reserved. Do a final proofread for any problems that may have crept in when you made changes. Double-check the numbering of items, sections, and pages. Electronically secure or anchor graphics so they don't "migrate" to unintended pages. No matter how good you believe your test is, always try it out on a human being before administering it to your actual target group. You may be surprised at certain results.

Be sure to back up the exam both electronically and in hard copies. Print the answer key or scoring sheet when you produce the exam. Keeping practicality in mind, produce the exam well in advance and store it securely. Nothing is more frustrating than a malfunctioning photocopy machine during exam week. Some textbook publishers now "bundle" computer-based testing (CBT) software such as ExamView® with their books. Such software is easy to use to create classroom or online tests. Tutorials typically accompany the software.

Preparing Students

Students need accurate information about assessment, and they need to develop good test-taking skills. In our coverage of the assessment process, we will focus on providing information to students since test-taking skills themselves are addressed in Chapter 7.

Transparency means that students have accurate information about when assessments will occur, what they will cover in terms of skills and material, how much the assessments are worth, and when students can reasonably get their results. If at all possible, provide an assessment schedule at the beginning of a school year or semester to hand out with the syllabus. Be clear but firm about due dates and policies regarding assessments not completed by those dates. For long-term assessments such as portfolios or projects, break down due dates into several interim dates instead of having the entire work due at once.

Many institutions now require students to have outcome statements from the beginning of a course of study so that they know what is expected of them. As you work through the syllabus, be sure to draw attention to these outcomes and clarify what they mean for students and what the consequences are of not meeting them. Point out that assessment tasks are designed to check that students have achieved the outcomes. Some teachers post outcomes in the classroom as a reminder of the goals to be achieved. Stress that the goals are achievable, and be positive about the progress students are making toward these goals.

Assessment in the Larger Cycle

In this book, we devote separate chapters to developing student test-taking skills (Chapter 7), the administration of assessment (Chapter 8), and techniques for analyzing exams (Chapter 9). Remember, assessment is part of a larger cycle so schedule time for analysis, feedback, and reflection. Administrators typically understand why we need time to prepare and grade examinations, but they need to see that we conduct assessment for several reasons that matter to all involved.

First, we want information about how our students are progressing. We want to confirm that they are placed at an appropriate level and are moving forward with their language skills. We want to give them the results of formative assessment as quickly as possible and make helpful suggestions for further improvement.

Second, we want to know whether our assessment instruments themselves are working for us. Do exams assess the skills we purport to teach? For example, if business students need telephone skills in the workplace, do we use performance assessment to check their skills? Do our assessment techniques yield useful information, or do we need to make some changes in how and what we assess?

Third, we want feedback about all aspects of our programs from syllabi to materials to instruction. Are the outcomes we have developed appropriate for our students? Are teachers able to cover material in the syllabus? Are the course materials performing as we had hoped or expected? If we notice that many students have problems in a particular area, what can we do to compensate? In general, have teaching techniques been effective in helping students to master material? If not, how could we make improvements? Good assessment can answer these questions, but only if we take the time to analyze results and communicate them to colleagues.

Last, assessment gives us a chance to take a big step and rethink our English program's current aims and whether they fit the needs of current students. Technological innovations push us to consider different goals and different ways of assessment. Twenty years ago, English language learners mostly dealt with printed texts, but today the Internet has changed all that. Now we have to consider whether our instruction provides students with the means to independently access Internet resources and evaluate whether or not they are germane. English viewed as an international language means that we no longer focus on native-speaker standards and imparting cultural information about places where English is the primary language. Instead, our focus is on clear communication in a global context. Clearly, assessment is a useful tool for evaluating program aims.

Ten Things to Remember about Developing Assessment

1. **Assessment is an integral part of the teaching/learning cycle.**
   It involves planning, development, administration, analysis, feedback, and reflection.

2. **Teachers are often involved with several phases of assessment at the same time.**
   It is not unusual to be analyzing a previous exam while you are writing new items.

3. **Transparency and accountability are the hallmarks of good assessment.**
   Be open about your rationale, your procedures, and your results.

4. **Specifications are tools that link learning outcomes with assessment instruments.**
   Use specifications to promote validity and reliability.

5. **Assessment development is a collegial activity.**
   Benefit from the contributions and feedback from your colleagues. Work together to review new items and guidelines for alternative assessment. Strive for consensus on marking.

6. **Prepare grading criteria and answer keys along with tests.**
   Thinking through grading issues clarifies ambiguous tasks and items at a stage when you can still remedy the situation. Don't wait until after giving an examination to develop answer keys.

7. **Professional development in assessment benefits everyone.**
   Schedule sessions on item writing, grading, analysis, and feedback to enhance skills.

8. **The cycle does not stop with obtaining grades. Schedule time for thorough analysis.**
   Get the most from your assessments by understanding how tests are performed.

9. **Provide feedback in a timely and accessible manner.**
   Tailor your feedback to your audience. Make feedback to students and administrators something they can actually use.

10. **Plan time for reflection on assessment.**
    Did your assessment serve its purpose well? Was it part of the students' learning experience? What improvements do you plan to make the next time? Write these things down so you don't forget them!

Extension Activity

Read about Mr. Knott's first exam experience and identify areas for improvement this year. As you read, circle or highlight problem areas. Then, compare your findings with those of Mr. Knott's colleague on page 15.

Mr. Knott's First Exam Experience

Mr. Knott, now in his second year of teaching, found his first year quite challenging. Last year, he taught in a different school where assessment did not receive much attention. In college, Mr. Knott took a testing course, but he still felt out of his element with assessment. He worried that if he admitted he didn't understand things like specifications that he would get a poor evaluation. He avoided assigning portfolios and projects since he didn't see the point of multiple measures of assessment. He based students' grades solely on the midterm and final exams.

As the date of the midterm exam approached, Mr. Knott still hadn't checked where he should be in the syllabus because he advocated a "just-in-time approach." He wanted to see what he <u>actually</u> had covered by the midterm exam date. A few days before the test date, Mr. Knott put together a midterm exam consisting of a reading from a well-known TOEFL® practice book, a written expression section from a grammar book that he used in college, and a listening activity from a recent unit in the students' textbook. He left out writing because he thought that the written expression section would suffice. He didn't want to leak details of the test, so he didn't supply students with information about the exam. Students were surprised by several new formats they had never encountered.

Mr. Knott made all formats objective to make grading easier. He had students swap papers in classes to grade some sections, and his wife helped him grade the rest. He did not use an answer key. Instead, when many students had difficulty with an item, he gave everyone full credit.

The scores were high, so Mr. Knott concluded that the test was good. He didn't do any analysis or reflect on how the test could give him feedback on his teaching. He was too busy to give students feedback or make notes about the exam. Besides, why would he want to change something that worked so well?

One of Mr. Knott's new colleagues had these comments and suggestions.

Mr. Sanchez's comments and suggestions

I was a new teacher not so long ago, and I remember being overwhelmed by all the things I was supposed to know about but really didn't. Mr. Knott is a talented teacher and open to constructive feedback, so I hope these suggestions are helpful to him.

Comments	Suggestions
He didn't understand specifications.	Specifications are really important in our assessment program, so I hope he will attend a workshop and get some experience using them.
He didn't see the point of multiple measures of assessment and based grades only on two exams.	Again, in our program we use many types of assessment, not just tests and quizzes. Feel free to ask your colleagues to show you examples of alternative assessment that work for them.
He didn't plan ahead or keep up with the syllabus.	This is a disservice to students because some will miss out on important material. In our lesson plans we have to show that we're on target. We schedule a whole range of regular assessments so our students get regular formative feedback.
He used material intended for different purposes and different course outcomes.	Without following specifications or mapping the actual course material, it is unlikely that these materials were relevant.
He used a listening activity that students had already heard and processed.	He didn't really test listening as a skill. Instead, he tested students' memories.
He left out assessment of writing.	In our program, the development of writing skills is very important. However, we assess it in many ways, so he needs to consult the writing specifications for details.
He failed to provide information to students who were subsequently surprised by new formats.	In our department, transparency is very important, so we inform students about what to expect. We always introduce new formats in a teaching context before using them in exams. Good assessment reflects actual teaching—both what was taught and how it was taught.
He didn't prepare an answer key in advance.	No wonder some items didn't work!
Students and his wife graded the exam.	There are some real security and reliability issues here, made worse by the absence of an answer key.
He didn't conduct analysis because of high scores.	The scores were inflated because of grading procedures. The students' difficulty with certain items indicated a real need for analysis.
He didn't give students feedback.	Assessment is part of the teaching/learning cycle, and students should learn from each assessment experience. They need feedback presented to them in a usable form.
He didn't have time for reflection, nor did he make any notes about the experience.	Fortunately, Mr. Knott seems to realize that this was not the way assessment should be developed. In our department, we set a time to talk about what we've learned from major assessments. I hope Mr. Knott will participate.

2 Techniques for Testing

Constructing test items and tasks for any type of assessment is a task filled with challenges. Why? Test items are the foundation of tests and the backbone of most assessment instruments.

With her exam specifications firmly in hand, Ms. Wright starts to prepare her midterm exam. In doing so, she does the following to ensure that her students are assessed fairly.

- She balances objective and subjective formats, ensuring that the ones she uses are familiar to students from classroom instruction.
- She derives the weightings in her exam from the focus in curricular outcomes.
- She strives for authentic use of target language through texts and communicative tasks with rich content.
- She has a colleague moderate her test and uses this to check timing, allowing three to four times the teacher's rate for students.
- She pilots her exam via a practice exam with similar rubrics, formats, content, and weighting.
- She plans to use the same basic test for different classes but randomizes questions and answers for objective items, and she writes a parallel prompt for subjective items.
- She gives students a clear idea of the number of points per section and expectations for writing to encourage good time management.

Classifying Test Items and Tasks

Test items can be classified in a number of ways. Some testers categorize items as *selection* and *supply* items. With selection items, a student selects the correct answer from a number of presented options. True/False, matching, and multiple choice are examples of selection items. With supply items, students must supply or construct the correct answer. Examples of supply items include short answer or completion, cloze, gap fill, and essay questions.

Teachers need to be aware of the implications for English language learners in choosing different test formats. The type of response can impact a student's ability to demonstrate what she or he actually knows or can do. For example, a student asked about the plot or sequence of a story might be entirely capable of selecting an appropriate answer. However, the same student with limited English may not be able to supply or create an answer that indicates that they actually understand the content of the story. This simple chart may help you decide what formats to use based on the ability of your students to supply their own answers.

Selection	True/False, Multiple Choice, Matching, Numbering Sequence
Supply	Cloze or Gap-Fill (no responses provided), Essay questions

Subjective or Objective Questions?

Items can also be classified by the way they are scored. Objective test items can be scored based only on following an answer key. Scoring objective items requires no expert judgment, specialist knowledge, or subjectivity on the part of the marker. Scoring subjective items, on the other hand, requires that the marker have knowledge of the content area being tested. Marking a subjective test frequently depends on impression, human judgment, and opinion at the time of the scoring.

In addition to the differences mentioned, subjective/objective item types have these characteristics.

Objective items are usually short answer–closed response items. These types of items test recognition mostly. Although they are usually quick and easy to grade, objective items are generally difficult to write well. In addition, if there are enough of them, they are quite reliable. The great majority of the workload for teachers who develop these items should take place <u>before</u> the test administration.

Subjective items usually require students to produce longer, more open-ended responses. The emphasis here is on *production,* as students are generally required to come up with an answer rather than select it from a list of alternatives. Subjective questions are generally easier to write than objective questions, but difficult and time consuming to mark. Objective items have relatively few response options while subjective items are open-ended so a lot of variation is possible in the responses. Reliability of subjective items can sometimes be problematic because these items require human scoring. Issues with inter-rater reliability are sometimes present in subjective-item types. For teachers who routinely use subjective items to test their students, the workload takes place <u>after</u> the test has been administered.

Objective test items are very popular with language teachers and test developers for two reasons. First, these items are easy and quick to mark. Second, they are flexible in that objective test items can be used to test both global and detailed understanding of a text or focus on specific areas of language like grammar and vocabulary. This chapter describes some of the most commonly used objective test items in English language testing, namely multiple choice questions (MCQ), True/False statements (T/F), and the matching format.

Multiple Choice Questions

Multiple choice questions (MCQs) are probably the most commonly used format in professionally developed tests. Teachers all over the world are familiar with the format from their own learning experience, and they understand how it works. Moreover, MCQs are widely used in textbooks as well as on high-profile English language proficiency exams. They are widely used to assess learning at the recall and comprehension levels. Although they are more difficult to write than True/False questions, the job becomes easier with the correct training and a little practice.

MCQs take many forms, but their basic structure is the stem and response. It is the test-taker's task to identify the correct or most appropriate choice. The *stem* is usually written as a question (i.e., *Where did John go?)* or an incomplete statement (i.e., *John* _____ *to the store).* The *response options* of an MCQ are the choices given to the test-taker. Typically, there are four choices when testing reading, vocabulary, and grammar, but just three with listening. Only three response options are recommended for listening assessment because students hear the input listening passage only once or twice. Four options put too much load on memory as well as require more reading when we are testing listening. The response options are most commonly expressed as A, B, C, and D. One of these response options is the *key* or correct answer. The others are referred to as *distractors* or incorrect response options. The purpose of distractors is to move students' attention away from the key if they do not know the correct answer, thus determining students' knowledge or skill.

The popularity of MCQs is based on several advantages associated with this format. First, if they are written well, they are very reliable because there is only one answer possible. Second, they can be useful at various educational levels—they are used to assess language at the elementary level and content associated with graduate-level language education. Third, assessment is not affected by test-takers' writing abilities because they are only required to circle the correct response, pencil in a bubble on a sheet, or click on the right answer option. In addition, MCQs are well liked by administrators as being a cost-effective format because they can be scored by computer if the institution has the correct equipment, which makes them quite easy to analyze. Last, students everywhere are familiar with this format.

However, there are some distinct disadvantages to using MCQs. The one most cited by teachers is that MCQs do not lend themselves to the testing of productive language skills or language as communication. Since they are often used to test recognition, teachers forget that they can also be used to assess higher-order thinking skills. Another disadvantage is that MCQs encourage guessing, which can have an effect on exam results. A fourth disadvantage, one that most teachers do not appreciate, is that it is challenging and time consuming to write plausible distracters and produce good items.

Common MCQ Item Violations

In presenting examples of the most common MCQ item violations, we suggest ways to repair them.

- *Grammatical inconsistency*

  A common mistake when developing MCQs is grammatical inconsistency between the stem and the response options. Almost always, the stem and the key are grammatically consistent, but distractors sometimes do not mesh properly with the stem.

  Jane spent most of the day at the mall, but she _____ anything.

  A. didn't buy
  B. bought
  C. not buy
  D. many shops

  In this item, of course, A is the key or answer. Distractor D is grammatically inconsistent with the other response options as it is a noun clause while the others are all verb forms. To fix this item, distractor D should be changed to a verb form like *buying.*

- *Extraneous cues or clues*

  Cueing can occur in two places on a test: within an item or within the test. An extraneous clue that occurs within the test is one where students can find the answer to a question somewhere else on the test paper in another section of the test. Consider the following cueing violation within an item:

  After I've had a big lunch, I only want an _____ for dinner.

  A. pot of soup
  B. apple
  C. big steak
  D. candy bar

  The key here is B because it is the only distractor that takes the article *an* in the stem. In this item, a student only needs to know the grammatical rules concerning *a* and *an* to figure out the correct response. To fix this item, consider putting *a/an* in the stem.

- *3 for 1 split*

  This item violation occurs when three distractors are parallel and one is not. It is sometimes called *odd man out*. This item violation varies in the degree of seriousness. It is a serious violation if the unparallel option is the key.

  > The company was in desperate need for more workers, so they _____ an expensive ad in the newspaper.
  >
  > A. placing
  > B. to place
  > C. placement
  > D. placed

In this item, D is the key. The 3 for 1 split is three verb forms (A, B, and D) and 1 noun (C). (As 3 for 1 splits go, this is not a terrible one because the key is not the odd man out, but often the odd man is the key.)

- *Impure items*

  Impure items are those that test more than one thing.

  > I didn't see _____.
  >
  > A. had the students gone
  > B. the students had gone
  > C. have the students gone
  > D. that students have gone

This item tests both verb tense and word order. Remember that good items should only test one concept or point.

- *Apples and oranges*

  An apples-and-oranges violation is one where two response options have no relation to the other two. This is often referred to as a 2 for 2 split. There are instances where 2 for 2 splits are acceptable (i.e., the case of opposites or affirmative/negative).

  > According to the reading passage, people use mobile phones _____.
  >
  > A. frequently
  > B. seldom
  > C. in their cars
  > D. for emergency purposes

Distractors A and B are adverbs and C and D are prepositional phrases. This item would be better if all the response options were either adverbs or prepositional phrases and only one was clearly the key. Without reference to the reading passage, all four options are potential keys.

- *Subsuming response options*

   In this item violation, the intended answer and a very good distractor could both be correct. Consider this sample listening item.

   > *Mary:* We need to buy some new lawn furniture so we can sit on the patio.
   >
   > *Steve:* Okay. I'll go to the mall tonight. Any special kind you're looking for?
   >
   > *Mary:* Something cheap and comfortable. Just don't get anything made of metal, please.

   What will Steve buy?

   - A. outdoor furniture
   - B. comfortable chairs
   - C. steel furnishings

   Although the key is B, it can be argued that A is correct on a higher level because *comfortable chairs* are part of *outdoor furniture*. It is a sign of a poor test item when two response options can be considered correct.

- *Unparallel options*

   This item violation occurs when the response options are not parallel either in length or in grammatical consistency.

   How do students in the suburbs usually travel to school?

   - A. by bus
   - B. they go by taxi
   - C. most of them either take the bus or get a lift from their parents
   - D. walk

   This item is not parallel in either grammar or in length. Distractor C is the key, and it is by far the longest response option. All response options should be the same part of speech and approximately the same length.

- *Gender bias in language*

Particular care should be taken when using vocabulary that relates to gender. For example:

My cousin works as a male nurse _____ General Hospital.

   A. over

   B. on

   C. from

   D. at

The term *nurse* refers to both men and women who work in this profession. We don't say "female teacher," so why the need to say "male nurse"?

- *Sensitivity*

Materials that have a negative emotional impact on students should be avoided. Similarly, test item content that could be upsetting or shocking to students is not advisable.

The _____ disaster of 2004 was the December 26th tsunami that struck southeast Asia.

   A. most worst

   B. baddest

   C. very bad

   D. worst

For a group of ESL students from Mexico, this item is not a problem. However, for students who might be from a country hit by the tsunami, this item could be very upsetting. Test-taking is a very scary experience for most students, so it is important that the content they encounter on tests not add to that fear.

- *Double answer or key*

This item violation is the most commonly made among teachers. It occurs when more than one response option is correct.

The teacher waited in her office until her students _____.

   A. came

   B. would come

   C. come

   D. had come

Many would argue that both A and D are correct responses.

- *No answer*

  This is a common item violation made by teachers. It occurs when the author of the test item forgets to include the key among the list of response options. This most often occurs when the item has undergone various revisions and rewrites.

  This is the restaurant _____ I told you about yesterday.

  A. what
  B. where
  C. why
  D. how

- *Giveaway distractors*

  This violation occurs when test-takers are able to improve their scores by eliminating absurd or giveaway distractors.

  According to the text, the author of the article comes from _____.

  A. Dubai
  B. France
  C. Buenos Aires
  D. Disneyland

  Students can easily eliminate D so it is not an effective distractor. It adds nothing to this question.

Tips for Writing Good Multiple Choice Questions

Multiple choice questions are the hardest type of objective question to write for classroom teachers. Teachers should keep the following guiding principles in mind when writing MCQs.

- **The question or task should be clear from the stem of the MCQ.**
  Write MCQs that test only one conccpt.

- **Take background knowledge into account.**
  The selection of the correct or best answer should involve interpretation of the passage/stem, not merely the activation of background knowledge.

- **Provide as much context as possible.**
  The MCQ format is often criticized for its lack of authenticity. Whenever possible, set items in context.

- **Keep sensitivity and fairness issues in mind.**
  It is important to write items that do not unfairly advantage or disadvantage certain groups of students. It is also crucial to avoid item content that could be offensive or upsetting.

- **Standardize the number of response options.**
  The optimum number of response options for foreign/second language testing is *four* for grammar, vocabulary, and reading, and *three* for listening. However, some testers feel that three response options are acceptable for classroom or progress testing. Although there is no psychometric advantage to having a uniform number (Frary, 1995), it is better to be consistent within a test.

- **One response option should be an unambiguous correct or best answer.**
  The three remaining options function as distractors. Distractors should attract students who are unsure of the answer.

- **All response options should be similar in length and level of difficulty.**
  Response options should be consistent with the stem and parallel in length and grammar with each other. Some teachers inadvertently make the answer longer and more detailed than the distractors

simply because they add information to make it unambiguously correct. Testwise students often spot this practice.

- **Avoid using distractors like *none of the above*, or *a, b, and sometimes c, but never d* options.**
  Avoid these because they test more than one thing at a time. The distractor *all of the above* is still acceptable in certain cases, but its use remains controversial. Those who are not in favor of it state that the recognition of two right options identifies it as the answer. Additionally, most teachers use it as the correct answer to almost every item containing it as a response option, and the test-wise student soon figures this out. Therefore, proponents of *all of the above* recommend using it as an incorrect answer as many times as a correct answer.

- **Correct answers should appear equally in all positions.**
  Randomly assign correct answers. Don't unconsciously introduce a pattern into the test that will help the students who are guessing or who do not know the answer to get the correct answer. Although it may make grading easier, it is a threat to reliability. Don't neglect placing the answer in the A position. Research has shown that this is the most neglected position because teachers want students to read through all response options before responding to the question, so teachers unconsciously place the actual answer further down in the list of response options. One way to randomize answers is to alphabetize them. By doing so, the correct answer will automatically vary in the A, B, C, or D position.

- **Move recurring information in response options to the stem.**
  If the same words appear in all response options, take these words out of the response options and put them in the stem.

- **Avoid writing absurd or giveaway distractors.**
  Do not waste space by including funny or implausible distractors in your items. All distractors should appear for a valid pedagogical reason.

- **Avoid extraneous clues.**
  Avoid unintentional grammatical, phonological, or morphological clues that assist students in answering an item without having the requisite knowledge or skill being tested.

- **Make the stem positive.**
  Writing the stem in the affirmative tends to make the question more understandable. Introducing negatives increases the difficulty and discrimination of the question. However, if you must make it negative, place the negative near the end of the statement (i.e., *Which of the following is NOT. . . . . .* or *All of the following are _____ except. . . .*).

- **Make sure all questions are independent of one another.**
  Avoid sequential items where the successful completion of one question presupposes a correct answer to the preceding question. This presents students with a double jeopardy situation. If they answer the first question incorrectly, they automatically miss the second question, thereby penalizing them twice.

- **Use statistics to help you understand your MCQs.**
  Statistics like item analysis can assist you in your decisions about items. Use statistics to help you decide whether to accept, discard, or revise MCQs. (See Chapter 9 for information on item analysis.)

True/False Format

True/False questions are second only to multiple choice questions in frequency of use in professionally produced tests and perhaps one of the most popular formats for teacher-produced tests. Basically, they are a specialized form of the MCQ format in which there are only two possible alternatives and where students must classify their answers into one of two response categories. The common response categories are: *True/False, yes/no, correct/incorrect, right/wrong,* or *fact/opinion*. Because True/False is the most common response category, these questions are generally referred to as True/False questions.

True/False questions are typically written as statements, and the students' task is to decide whether they are True or False. They are attractive to many test developers because they offer several advantages. First, when you use this question type, you can test large amounts of content. Additionally, because True/False questions are shorter than most other item types, they typically require less time for students to respond to them. Consequently, more items can be incorporated into tests than is possible with other item types, which increases reliability. Another big advantage is that scoring is quick and reliable and can be accomplished efficiently and accurately.

Despite their advantages, True/False questions have several disadvantages. One is that there is a 50 percent guessing factor that the choice will be correct. With only two possible answers, there is always the danger that guessing may distort or inflate the final mark. To overcome this disadvantage, it is recommended that teachers use a third response category called Not Given or Not Enough Information. By doing so, the guessing factor goes from 50 percent to a more acceptable 33.3 percent. Yet another way to alleviate this problem is to ask students to correct false statements or to find statements in the text that support either a true or a false response. These two methods increase the diagnostic value of True/False questions. A second disadvantage of True/False items is that for them to be reliable, you need to include a sufficient number of them on the test.

Teacup Dogs

Teacup dogs are the latest must-have Hollywood fashion accessory. They get their name because these tiny dogs fit rather nicely into a teacup. The latest Hollywood trend weighs less than three pounds. You only need to flip through the pages of celebrity magazines to see these adorable dogs peeking out of designer handbags on the streets of New York and Hollywood. A trend originally started by Paris Hilton's Chihuahua, Tinkerbell, now other celebrities proudly sport tiny dogs as fashion accessories.

Animal cruelty activists, however, state that this fashion statement has gone too far. They point out that due to increased pressure from buyers, breeders are attempting to downsize these dogs still further. Because of these breeding practices, these darling dogs are often unhealthy creatures. Veterinarians point out that teacup dog owners have to cope with high medical bills as teacup dogs are prone to genetic diseases like water on the brain, heart problems, knee problems, and dental disease. Even more sadly, this wide range of medical problems causes them to have a shorter life span than normal dogs.

So are teacup dogs the latest fashion statement or an example of cruelty to animals? You decide.

Answer the following questions.

Poor T/F question: Teacup dogs weigh less than three pounds.

Better T/F question: Teacup dogs are much smaller than normal dogs.

The first question is more or less a verbatim matching from the text. The latter option is better as it paraphrases the information.

Poor T/F question: Teacup dogs are only found in New York and Hollywood.

The word *only* in the first option is an absoluteness clue to this sentence being false as you only need one exception (in this case one other teacup dog in another city) to make it false.

Poor T/F question: The author of this article is probably a proponent of teacup dogs.

Better T/F question: The author of this article probably likes teacup dogs.

The word *proponent* in the first option makes this question very difficult. An easier synonym like *supporter* is less difficult but still assesses the same principle. Simplifying vocabulary ensures that you are testing a target concept, not the confounding vocabulary in the question itself. This attention to potentially problematic vocabulary is especially important to K–12 audiences.

Tips for Writing Good True/False Questions

The following tips can help you write effective True/False questions.

- **Write items that test meaning rather than trivial detail.**
  True/False items are said to test gist or intensive understanding very well.

- **Questions should be written at a lower level of language difficulty than the text.**
  This is important because you want to ensure that comprehension is based on understanding of the text and not understanding of the question itself. (This is important for lower-proficiency learners, especially K–12 learners.)

- **Consider the effects of background knowledge.**
  Successful completion of True/False/Not Given items should depend on the students' reading of the text, not on background knowledge.

- **Questions should appear in the same order as the answers appear in the text.**
  By mixing the order of True/False questions in reading and listening, you increase the difficulty of these questions significantly.

- **Make sure you paraphrase questions in simple, clear language.**
  It is better to paraphrase questions rather than take them verbatim from the text. The latter only requires students to locate the relevant statements in the text to be able to answer them. Paraphrase by using vocabulary and grammar from course materials. The language of the question should be simple and clear yet have sufficient information to allow its truthfulness to be judged.

- **Avoid absoluteness clues.**
  Do not use specific determiners like *all, none, always,* and *never.* Questions with these determiners are easy because the answer is most always false. Similarly, avoid determiners like *sometimes* and *some* as they tend to appear in statements that are true.

- **Focus each item on a single idea from the text.**
  Items that require students to deal with the possible truth or falsity of two or more ideas at once increase the difficulty of the question substantially.

- **Avoid answer patterns.**
  Don't be tempted to write questions with a specific answer pattern like TTFFTTFFTT to facilitate your grading. Students will soon catch on to these tactics. Answer patterns in your questions should not be discernable.

- **Include enough questions.**
  True/False questions are a reliable way of testing students' comprehension if there are enough items. It is recommended that teachers include a minimum of seven to ten questions on their tests when using this format.

- **Add a third option to decrease the guessing factor.**
  The True/False format has a high guessing factor. By adding a third response category (Not Given or Not Enough Information), teachers can decrease this guessing factor. It should be noted that the NG/NI option is appropriate for students at the intermediate level and

higher and should not be used in the assessment of listening comprehension. In reading comprehension, students have unlimited opportunities to go back to the text to determine if content is not given, but
in listening comprehension, students hear the source text only once
or twice. Including an NG option would tax students' memory.

- **Have students circle T, F, or N on the test paper or answer
  sheet.**
  By doing so, you will avoid getting those Ts that suspiciously look
  like Fs. This will substantially facilitate your marking.

Matching Format

Another common objective format is matching. Matching is an extended form
of MCQ that draws on the student's ability to make connections among ideas,
vocabulary, and structure. Matching questions present the students with two
columns of information. Students must find the matches between the two
columns. Items in the left-hand column are called *premises* or stems, and the
items in the right-hand column are called *options*. The advantage of matching
questions over MCQs is that the student has more distractors per item. Additionally, writing items in the matching format is somewhat easier for teachers
than either MCQs or True/False/Not Given.

Consider this example assessing proverbs.

Poor Matching Question Set:

1. better late	A. wear it
2. if the shoe fits,	B. keeps the doctor away
3. an apple a day	C. is not gold
4. the early bird	D. catches the worm
5. all that glitters	E. than never

Both the options and the premises have an equal number of choices. Therefore
if students miss one, they miss at least two automatically. Similarly, if they get
four correct, they get the last one correct by default. When formatting matching
questions, it is better to draw a line before the numbers so that students can
write "the letter of the correct answer in the space provided." With no blanks,
in order to answer students will have to draw lines from option to premise,
making grading very difficult.

Consider this better example that asks students to match useful expressions with context of their use.

_____ 1. when you are introduced to someone new   A. I'm sorry.

_____ 2. to apologize to someone   B. Stop it.

_____ 3. you don't know the answer to a question   C. Nice to meet you.

_____ 4. when you are joking with someone   D. I've got it.

E. I'm just kidding.

F. I give up.

In this example, there are two more options than premises which function as distractors. To answer the questions, students have space to write the answer in the space provided thus facilitating the grading process for teachers.

Tips for Writing Matching Items

These are some important points to bear in mind when writing matching questions:

- **Give more options than premises.**
  Never write items that rely on direct 1-on-1 matching. The consequence of 1-on-1 matching is that if a student gets one item wrong, at least two (but potentially many more) are wrong by default. By contrast, if the student gets all previous items right, the last item is a process of elimination "freebie."

- **Number the premises and letter the options.**
  To facilitate marking, number the premise column and letter the option column. Then have students write the *letter of the correct answer in the space provided.*

- **Make options shorter than premises.**
  When developing matching questions, write options that are relatively short. This will reduce the reading load on the part of students.

- **Options and premises should be related to one central theme.**
  Relating the information in both columns to one central theme will make for a more coherent test section.

- **Avoid widows.**

  "Widows" occur when half of a test section or question overlaps onto another page. Make sure the matching section (and all other sections) on your test is all on the same page. Students might fail to see any answer items that continue on another page.

- **Make it clear to students if they can use options more than once.**

  Be sure to explicitly state in the rubric whether options can be used more than once. If this is not permitted, you might advise students to cross out options they have already used.

- **Ask students to write the letter of the correct answer in a blank provided.**

  Failure to include this in the rubric will force students to draw lines between options and premises making them next to impossible to grade.

Cloze/Gap-Fill Items

This section discusses common subjective items used on language tests: cloze and gap fill, short answer and completion items, and essay questions. Many teachers don't distinguish between gap fill and cloze tests. However, there are some important differences between the two. In gap-fill questions, we normally choose the words that we delete, whereas in cloze, we delete the words systematically.

Cloze testing originated in the 1950s as a test of reading comprehension. Conventional cloze tests involve the removal of words at regular intervals, usually every six to eight words and normally not less than every five. The student's task is to complete the gaps with appropriate fillers. To do this, students have to read around the gap. More specifically, they must refer to the text on either side of the gap, taking into account meaning and structure to process the answer. Although they remain primarily a test of reading, cloze formats can test a wide variety of language areas.

In gap-fill items, a word or phrase is replaced by a blank in a sentence. The student's task is to fill in the missing word or phrase. Harrison (1983) identifies two types of gap fills: function gaps (such as prepositions, articles, conjunctions) that have only one correct filler, and semantic gaps (such as nouns, adjectives, verbs, and adverbs) that can be filled with a number of different alternatives (p. 40). Rational deletion cloze is similar to gap fill in that specific categories of words have been deleted for assessment purposes. See an example in Chapter 3 on page 53.

Tips for Writing Cloze/Gap-Fill Items

- **Ensure that answers are concise.**
  The response that goes in the blank should not be overly long. Make sure there is enough room in the blank to comfortably write the response.

- **Provide enough context.**
  There needs to be sufficient context present for students to surmise what goes in the blank.

- **Blanks should be of equal length.**
  When putting blanks in your paragraph/text, make sure they are the same length. Providing blanks that differ in length implies responses of varying lengths. The main body of the question should precede the blank.

- **Develop and allow for a list of acceptable responses.**
  When grading cloze/gap fill items, be sure to allow for the possibility of more than one answer.

- **Don't put a gap in the first sentence of a paragraph or text.**
  Normally the initial sentence in a paragraph or text is used to set the context for the reading to follow. Including questions in this part of the text can be problematic for students.

Short Answer/Completion Items

Short answer or sentence completion items ask students to answer in a few words, phrases, or sentences. These items offer a number of advantages. First, they encourage students to learn and know the answer rather than just recognize it. Second, because students must produce the answer, there is less guessing. Third, they are easy to construct. Fourth, they are especially good for checking gist, intensive understanding of a text, and *who, what, where,* and *when* content. Finally, these question types can test higher-order thinking skills.

Teachers also point out a number of disadvantages to short answer/sentence completion items. One disadvantage is that responses may take the student longer, which reduces the possible number of items on a test. Second, the student has to produce language to respond, and this may discourage the rote memorization of facts. Issues having to do with scoring are perhaps the most cited disadvantage with this item format. Because there is often a significant amount of language to assess, scoring may take longer. Since the scoring is subjective, it has the potential to be unreliable through *inter-rater* and *intra-rater* reliability issues. Inter-rater reliability refers to the consistency between two or more graders. Intra-rater reliability refers to one grader's inner consistency between one marking session and another.

Tips for Writing Short Answer/Completion Items

- **There should be only one short, concise answer.**
  Responses that are short and concise are easier to grade. Teachers should specify the number of words if there is a limit.

- **Allow for partial credit.**
  Teachers should consider the issue of partial credit for answers that have varying degrees of correctness. A major goal of testing/assessment is giving students credit for what they know.

Essay Questions

Essay questions offer students the greatest opportunity to construct their own responses. With this question type, it is the student who decides how to approach the question, which ideas to include, how to organize these points, and which conclusions to make. Essay questions are the most useful format for assessing higher-order cognitive processes such as analyzing, evaluating, summarizing, and synthesizing.

Despite these advantages, essay questions are time consuming for students to answer, thereby allowing for the testing of only a limited amount of student learning. Essay questions not only assess content knowledge, they place a premium on writing ability. Since essay questions are scored subjectively, there is the potential for reliability problems. For teachers the scoring workload is the biggest disadvantage to using the essay question format.

Tips for Writing Essay Questions

- **Make all questions similar in level of difficulty.**
  This is especially important if students are given a selection of essay questions and have to choose the ones they answer. If the questions vary in difficulty, students will go for the easier ones.

- **Write questions that force students to use higher-order thinking skills.**
  Use essay questions to their best advantage by requiring students to use higher-order cognitive processes such as analyzing, evaluating, summarizing, and synthesizing by using verbs such as compare and contrast, defend, support, and predict.

- **Allow students enough space to write their answer.**
  Leave sufficient space (preferably lined) for students to plan and write their answer. Have extra lined paper on hand during the exam in case students need to continue or double space their answers.

- **Be specific in the amount or type of information you want in the answer.**
  If you want students to include specific information in their answers, tell them in the prompt. If a specific number of paraphrases or pages is required, include that information as well. Be clear about the number of examples you require or if students are expected to give their own opinion.

- **Assess content selectively.**
  Sometimes content is better suited to another format. Assess only content that is appropriate with this format.

- **Share the scoring rubric with students prior to the exam.**
  Develop a specified scoring rubric and then share and discuss this rubric with your students before (or even during) the exam. Transparency will help decrease student anxiety.

Ten Things to Remember about Testing Techniques

1. **Design tests and assessment tasks based on blueprints or test specifications.**
   It is easier to create parallel items/tasks if test developers follow a blueprint or test specification. If you don't have a test specification but do have an assessment task that works, analyze what the task entails and write a specification to fit it.

2. **Ensure the format remains the same within one section of the exam.**
   It is confusing to mix formats within the same section of a test.

3. **Make sure the item format is correctly matched to the test purpose and course content.**
   Test items should relate to curricular objectives. Teachers should think about what they are trying to test and match their purpose with the item format that most closely resembles it.

4. **Include items of varying levels of difficulty.**
   Present items of different levels of difficulty throughout the test from easy to difficult. We recommend the 30/40/30 principle. When constructing a test, try to direct 30 percent of the questions to the below average students in the class, 40 percent of the questions to those who have mid-range abilities, and the remaining 30 percent of the questions should be directed toward those students who are above average in their language ability. In this way, everyone in the class, no matter what their ability level, will have access to some of the questions.

5. **Start with an easy question first.**
   If you follow the 30/40/30 principle mentioned, start the exam with one of the questions from the easy group. This will relax students, which will lower their anxiety levels.

6. **Avoid ambiguous items, negatives, and especially double negatives.**
   Unless your purpose as a tester is to test ambiguity, avoid ambiguous items. Sometimes ambiguous language causes students to answer incorrectly even when they know the answer. Negatives and double negatives are extremely confusing and should be avoided; if the intention is to test negatives, only relevant information should be presented.

7. **Avoid race, gender, and ethnic background bias.**
   Sometimes test content unfairly biases certain groups. To avoid this, examine your items carefully. Make sure that at least one other colleague has looked over your items to check for bias.

8. **Prepare answer keys in advance of test administration.**
   Develop keys and model answers at the same time you develop the test or assessment task.

9. **Employ items that test all levels of thinking.**
   Avoid lifting items verbatim from test stimulus. This does not require a great deal of processing from our students. Try to include items/tasks of varying degrees of sophistication and levels of thinking. Remember the six levels in Bloom's Taxonomy (1984): Knowledge, Comprehension, Application, Analysis, Synthesis, and Evaluation.

10. **Give clear instructions.**
    When we assess our students, we want to know if they comprehend the questions we are asking them. Directions that are too elaborate, for example, could impede student comprehension, thereby skewing test results.

Extension Activity

Mr. Knott has just developed his midterm English exam for his integrated skills ESL class. Look at the grammar and vocabulary section and decide which aspects of his test are good. What could be done to improve the test? Compare your comments to what some colleagues had to say about Mr. Knott's test (pages 40–42).

English Midterm Grammar Exam

Directions: Questions 1–10 are in complete sentences. Choose the best word or phrase to complete each sentence. Indicate the correct letter (10 points total; 1 point each).

1. Obet lives in Detroit. _____ works in the auto industry.
   a. her
   b. he
   c. him
   d. she

2. My sister _____ as an air hostess.
   a. working
   b. works
   c. she works
   d. job

3. Tuesday and Wednesday come before Thursday but after
   _____
   a. Sunday
   b. Saturday
   c. Monday
   d. Friday
   e. None of the above

4. I'm hungry. I think I'll eat an _____
   a. orange juice
   b. fork
   c. éclair
   d. automobile

5. The answer to question three is the _____ day of the week.
   a. first
   b. forth
   c. three
   d. fifth

6. I usually participate in the regatta _____ June.
   a. from
   b. on
   c. at
   d. to

7. Juan is a lazy person. He usually takes a siesta _____ the weekend.
   a. on
   b. during
   c. at
   d. throughout

8. Although the proposal has some disadvantages, they are outweighed by the _____.
   a. advantages
   b. negatives
   c. drawbacks
   d. problem

9. While my mother prepared the _____ for dinner, I watched television.
   a. kitchen
   b. children
   c. chicken
   d. cartoon

10. An architect is a person who does not _____.
    a. design automobiles
    b. design buildings
    c. design houses
    d. design offices

11. Can you type _____ on a computer?
    a. typing
    b. to type
    c. typed
    d. type

Mr. Knott's Grammar and Vocabulary Test— A Critical Review

Good Things:

- Directions aren't too bad.
- Point values for the section and each question are indicated

Problem Areas:

- Directions:
  —Typo: should read *incomplete* (one word) instead of *in complete*.
  —*Indicate the correct letter* is not precise enough; should state *how* students will indicate it. Do they *circle the letter of the correct answer, write the letter of the correct answer on the answer sheet provided,* or *write the letter of the correct answer in the blank?*
  —There are, in fact, 11 questions, not 10. The extra question could be an issue. Do we add a point for the section or delete one of the questions? If so, which question should we delete?

- Test Items:
  —Question 1:
    › Is Obet a male or a female? When testing gender-specific subject pronouns, it is better to use a name that all students are familiar with.
    › Since the blank is in sentence initial position, all response options need to begin with a capital letter.
  —Question 2:
    › 3-for-1 split item violation (3 = *working, works, she works*; 1 = *job*).
    › Inappropriate terminology item violation: The term *air hostess* is dated, and some would argue that it is politically incorrect; a better term here would be *flight attendant*.
    › Response option *c* is a commonly made mistake among several language groups (i.e., Arab speakers, etc.); in heterogeneously grouped classes where there are several different language groups represented, this could be viewed as entrapment.
  —Question 3:
    › This is a confusing way to assess days of the week and sequencing.
    › Impure item as it tests both days of the week and sequencing.

> More than one response option is keyable.
> Use of five response options is not consistent with other questions.
> The first day of the week in many countries is Monday. However, in the Arab world, the first day of the week is Sunday.
> Use of *None of the above* should be avoided.

—Question 4:

> Extraneous clue item violation: the use of *an* in the stem is a clue that only three response options work.
> Response option D *(automobile)* is a giveaway distractor.
> If students know that *juice* is something you drink, they can easily eliminate A as an answer.
> As such, students can figure out that C *(éclair)* is the key without really knowing what it means.
> Surely there is another more high-frequency noun that could be used in place of *éclair*.

—Question 5:

> 3-for-1 split item violation (3 ordinal numbers = *first, fourth, fifth;* 1 roman numeral = *three*).
> Presupposed knowledge item violation: The successful completion of this question is linked to the successful completion of Question 3. Therefore, if the student has missed Q3, then he/she automatically misses Q5. This is known as a double jeopardy.
> Typo: *forth* should be written as *fourth*.

—Question 6:

> No key item violation: Key is not among the list of response options.
> The term *regatta* is a word associated with affluent people. Perhaps a term like *boat race* would be more accessible to the average student.

—Question 7:

> Double key item violation: Both *on* and *at* (British English) *the weekend* are acceptable. One could also argue that *during* and *throughout* are possible.
> Stereotype item violation: The association of a Hispanic name with taking a siesta promotes a stereotype.

—Question 8:

> 3-for-1 split item violations: (3 plurals/1 singular or 3 negative words and 1 positive). The latter is the most serious type of 3-for-1 split because the odd man out (*advantages*) is the key.
> There is a collocation between *advantages* and *disadvantages*, which could be counted as an extraneous clue.

—Question 9:

> Multiple key violations: Arguably, A, B, and C could fit and make sense.

—Question 10:

> Use of the word *not* increases the difficulty on this question so much that it is even difficult for native speakers.
> We don't often define a person/profession by what he or she does not do.
> The word *design* should be moved to the stem.

—Question 11:

> Answer *type* has been left in the stem.

- Test as a whole:
  > Grammar and vocabulary should be tested in separate sections.
  > Grammar questions outnumber vocabulary items.
  > No real sense of cohesion as to what the main grammar points are.
  > For more reliable results, more than 10 questions should be included.

3 Assessing Reading

It is difficult to assess an invisible skill, but that is exactly the dilemma language teachers face when they test their students' abilities in reading (and listening). We cannot actually see what is going on in students' minds when they read (or listen), so we design assessment based on *constructs* or models of receptive skills that include a variety of subskills. This chapter examines current ideas about reading—including its subskills and strategies—before exploring techniques for assessment.

How important is reading in your school's assessment of your learners?		
(A) **Intensive English Program, Community College, University (-Bound) Program:** Reading is fundamental to academic success and is a major component of any type of assessment. Because reading is crucial to post-secondary academic success, the TOEFL® (Test of English as a Foreign Language), which is required for admission to most North American colleges and universities, gives heavy weight to reading.	(B) **Conversation Classes, Non-academic Programs, Survival Classes:** Reading is not important and is rarely tested. However, learners need a certain level of reading ability to take whatever exams the program may have.	(C) **K–12:** Reading is the backbone of most overall assessments, including statewide assessments, that all K–12 students must take. Teachers need to consider how certain question types may negatively impact ELLs scores regardless of their language proficiency. In addition, they should make an extra effort to familiarize their learners with the format and directions of the examination.

Reading is a key skill for Ms. Wright's English language learners. Her school is eager to improve reading results on state and national examinations, so administrators asked for a report of what Ms. Wright does to assess her students' reading abilities. Some of the things she does to ensure valid and reliable reading assessment are:

- She covers a range of reading skills from gist comprehension to scanning for detail and inferencing for implied information.
- She chooses different text topics and types and uses several passages per test.
- She employs a range of different task types but ensures that students are familiar with them.
- She expects students to distinguish between main ideas and supporting details.
- She asks students to infer the meaning of unfamiliar words from context.
- She treats grammar as an important part of reading comprehension.
- She tests discourse-level aspects of texts, including text types and discourse markers.
- She asks students to recognize the purposes and audiences of texts.
- She encourages critical-thinking skills such as distinguishing fact from opinion.

Approaches to Reading

What exactly is *reading?* In daily life, we certainly encounter a wide range of reading material and tasks, yet it is difficult to define exactly what we mean by *reading.* Is reading mainly taking in new information, or is it a process of synthesizing new information with what we already know? Is reading a matter of decoding symbols to form words and sentences, or is it understanding how arguments are presented and recognizing typical texts used for certain purposes, such as a narrative story or assembly instructions for a bookcase? In fact, when we think of texts, do we think of prose passages, or do we consider advertisements, maps, graphs, and cartoons as texts, too?

Today, most English language teachers would agree that reading includes both bottom-up skills—recognizing and making sense of letters, words, and sentences—and top-down processing that deals with whole texts. They would also agree that *text* applies to both linear passages of prose as well as a wide variety of non-linear sources of information such as maps and pie charts. Reading is widely regarded as an interactive skill in which the background knowledge or schemata that the reader brings to the task is constantly interwoven with the new material. There are many processes involved in reading, but also important are products or results of reading.

With a skill as complex as reading, it is challenging to choose what to assess. In his comprehensive overview of reading assessment, Alderson (2000) argues that the place to start is the target skills we want our students to develop. In a particular teaching setting, what kind of reading do students need to do, and what subskills and strategies are important in that context? If you are teaching ELLs in K–12, what reading skills do your students need? Alderson sees the construct of reading as a mental model that translates more abstract theories of reading ability into tasks that can be operationalized in assessment (p. 117). Once we have defined the construct of reading that applies to our teaching situation and its curricular outcomes, we can then move on to designing reading specifications for assessment.

Reading Subskills

Most language teachers assess reading through the component subskills. Since it is not possible to observe reading behavior directly, we can only get an idea of how students actually process texts through techniques such as think-aloud protocols. For classroom assessment, we normally focus on certain important skills that can be divided into major and minor (or contributing) reading skills. These categories are based on whether the skills pertain to large segments of the text or focus on local structural or lexical points.

Major reading skills include:

- reading quickly to skim for gist, scan for specific details, and establish overall organization of the passage
- reading carefully for main ideas, supporting details, author's argument and purpose, relationship of paragraphs, and fact versus opinion
- information transfer from nonlinear texts
- drawing inferences from both stated and implied content

Minor or enabling reading skills include:

- understanding at the sentence level
  —vocabulary, syntax, cohesive markers
- understanding at inter-sentence level
  —identifying what pronouns refer to, recognizing discourse markers
- understanding components of nonlinear texts
  —the meaning of graph or chart labels, keys, and the ability to find and interpret intersection points

Vocabulary and Grammar

Increasingly, grammar and vocabulary are contextualized as part of reading passages instead of being assessed separately in a discrete point fashion. For example, older versions of the TOEFL® examination contained a grammar editing section where the students had to identify grammar errors. In the most recent version of the TOEFL® (iBT), language skills are integrated, and grammar is subsumed within other skills. Similarly, vocabulary is tested within context in each of the skills. In other words, a student's skills in these areas are assessed as they produce written and spoken responses.

However, there are times when it is appropriate to assess structure and vocabulary separately. Some testers such as Hughes (2003, p. 138) advocate separate testing of grammar and vocabulary because of the washback effect on learning if these underlying skills themselves are not tested (pp. 172-179). Remember, washback is the influence of testing on teaching and learning. If you stress something in teaching, but you do not assess it, students get a mixed message about its importance. Vocabulary research has shown that language learners benefit from both explicit instruction and incidental learning (Folse, 2004), so if your program includes an explicit vocabulary-building component, it clearly makes sense to assess it separately.

Considerations in Designing Tasks

Reading tests use many of the formats discussed in Chapter 2. Recognition or selective-response formats include multiple choice questions (MCQs), true/false/not given (T/F/NGs), and matching and cloze—all formats where the student selects from a range of provided answers. When we move to gap-fill or short answer formats, students must produce an answer. With these limited production formats, remember that the emphasis is generally on meaning. If it is clear that the student understood the task, mechanical mistakes such as spelling that do not interfere with meaning should not be graded as wrong. However, for authentic tasks such as reading directions for filling in a form, accuracy is important.

Increasingly, commercial examinations like TOEFL® or the Cambridge ESOL exams such as FCE (First Certificate in English) use formats that require students to deal with the text as a whole. In some cases, students are asked to insert missing sentences into appropriate places in the text. In other cases, they are asked to order chunks of texts or paragraphs to demonstrate their understanding of sequence or text organization. Some integrative exams require students to write a summary or response to texts they have read.

Specifications

Specifications help teachers and administrators establish a clear link between the overall objectives for the program and the design of particular assessment instruments. Specifications are especially useful for ensuring even coverage of the main skills and course content as well as developing tests that are comparable to one another because they are based on the same guidelines. Some typical features of specifications are:

- content
- conditions
- grading criteria

Content

- What material will the test cover? What aspects of this material? For example, if you teach a content-based course, will the material cover topics similar to those that students have already encountered? Will it recycle vocabulary that students know as well as test unknown vocabulary in context?
- What does the student have to be able to do? Will students demonstrate prediction or other prereading skills? You may decide that it is important to spend class time developing certain reading skills or strategies but impractical to assess all of

them. You must decide what to prioritize in terms of your curriculum and the needs of your students.

- Specifications often state the type and number of texts (prose or non-linear), the number of words in the passage, and readability level.

Conditions

- Specifications usually provide information about the structure of the examination and the component parts. For example, a reading examination may include five subsections that use different formats and texts to test different subskills.
- Specific formats or a range of formats are usually given in specifications in addition to the number of questions for each format or section. It is strongly advisable to have four to ten items for each format because changing formats too frequently can be disruptive.
- Decide whether students will have access to the text(s) as they answer questions. Under some circumstances, such as skimming for gist comprehension, you might lay out the test so that students quickly read the text, then turn a page and answer comprehension questions.
- Timing is another condition that is included in specifications. The time may be given for the entire test or each individual subsection. For example, you can place time-dependent skills such as skimming and scanning in separately timed sections, or you can place them at the end of a longer reading test where students typically read faster to finish within the allocated time.

Grading Criteria

- Specifications indicate how the assessment instrument will be marked. For instance, the relative importance of marks for communication contrasted to those for mechanics (spelling, punctuation, capitalization) should reflect the overall approach and objectives of the instructional program. Similarly, if some skills are deemed more important or require more processing than others, they may be weighted more heavily.

Some sample specifications for two reading tasks based on the same text, one using MCQs and the other using the T/F/NG format are provided.

Sample Specifications

Sample Reading Specifications

Total Marks: 50

Time: 30 MINUTES
Part 1

Text Type	TEXT A Descriptive or narrative text, authentic or modified
Advanced Level English for Academic Purposes (EAP)	Text length: 500 words Flesch-Kincaid Grade Level 10–11
Topic	Based on topics covered in course materials (so students have background knowledge and familiarity with vocabulary)
Skills	Gist comprehension, main ideas, supporting details, reference, vocabulary in context, text coherence
Task	5 Multiple Choice items with 4 options each, one of which is the key; questions within this section will appear in order of the text with the exception of the placement item. Ensure that there are two distractors in the text for each item.

Skill Focus of Individual Items	The items should be written as follows:
	  a. Item requires finding factual information in the text at the sentence level.
	  b. Item asks students to identify across-sentence boundaries, the referent of a subject, object or possessive pronoun (highlighted or paragraph given).
	  c. Item about the meaning of an unknown word in context (word highlighted or line given).
	  d. Item requires identification of a main idea at either the paragraph or whole text level (title, topic for paragraph, etc.).
	  e. Item requires choice of appropriate sentence for placement at Δ symbol. Distractor sentences should sample the entire text, and the question should appear at end of section.

Marking	5 marks per item, no partial scores, students circle letter of answer.

Part 2

Text Type	Use TEXT A (see Part 1)
Level	See Part 1
Topic	See Part 1

Skills	Reading comprehension requiring higher-order thinking skills than required in Part 1. Items should require that students:
	    a. process information beyond the sentence level
	    b. understand paraphrased wording
	    c. understand the difference between accurate and inaccurate information and information not provided by the text itself
	    d. recognize the purpose, bias, or intended audience of the author

Task	5 True/False/Not Given items where students circle answer. Wording of the statements must be positive.

Skill Focus of Individual Items	The five T/F/NG items must test the following abilities:
	    a. connect information in different parts of a paragraph
	    b. connect information in different parts of the text
	    c. identify paraphrased ideas from the text
	    d. recognize what information is actually given in the text and differentiate it from background knowledge
	    e. identify the attitude, opinion, or purpose of the writer

Note:	There must be at least one T, F, and NG as the correct responses, but only one NG item per section.
Marking	5 marks per item, no partial scores, students circle letter of answers

Texts

There are many sources for reading texts. Texts can be purpose written, taken directly from authentic material, or adapted. The best way to develop good reading assessments is to constantly watch for appropriate material. Keep a file of authentic material from newspapers, magazines, brochures, instruction guides—any suitable source of real texts. You can find material on particular topics in an encyclopedia written at an appropriate readability level or use an Internet search engine. Whatever source you use, cite it properly on the exam paper as a model for students. An exception would be when you have a question about the source of the text, such as, *Where would you find this reading?* with supplied responses such as *an encyclopedia, a dictionary, a telephone book, a guidebook,* etc. Another exception would be if the information is publicly available in many sources.

Reading texts include both prose passages and non-linear texts such as tables, graphs, schedules, maps, advertisements, and diagrams. Whenever possible, present them in a realistic manner. For instance, a scanning task might involve reading six or seven short advertisements similar to those in the classified section of a newspaper. Be sure that all texts are clear and legible.

Avoid texts with controversial or biased material. For example, do not use a paragraph on religion, abortion, or international disputes. Although such texts might generate enthusiastic classroom discussions, they are not suitable for assessment because they can upset students and affect the reliability of test results. Remember that texts should be as culturally neutral as possible to avoid offense. To this end, people in a passage should not be drinking alcohol, dating, or discussing any taboo subjects.

You should check the language of your reading texts. This can be done quite easily with Microsoft® Word, which provides word counts and readability statistics. First, highlight the passage, then select Word Count from the Tools menu. To access readability information, go to Options under the Tools menu, choose the Spelling and Grammar tab, and check Show Readability Statistics. Readability is based on word and sentence length as well as use of the passive voice. You can raise or lower the level by changing these. You can also add line numbers and other special features to texts. This is very useful if you wish to refer to a word in a particular line. Ninety percent of the vocabulary in a prose passage should already be known to the students for good comprehension (Nation, 1990).

Questions

Make sure that your questions are written at a slightly lower level than the reading passages. Reading comprehension questions should be in the same order as the material in the passage itself. Mixing up the order of questions substantially increases the difficulty level. If you have two types of questions or two formats based on one text, go through the text with different colored markers to check that you have evenly covered the material in sequence.

For objective formats such as MCQ and T/F/NG, make all statements positive. If you phrase a statement negatively and an option is negative as well, students have to deal with the logical problems of double negatives. Whenever possible, rephrase material using synonyms to avoid students scanning for verbatim matches. Paraphrasing encourages vocabulary growth as positive washback.

Formats

At the most basic levels of second language literacy, it may be important to focus on decoding skills and the ability to recognize letters and words. H. D. Brown (2004) points out that this is a special concern for immigrants whose first language uses a different script or who may not have been literate in that language (p. 190). Assessment of early literacy is best accomplished with the simplest formats that involve minimal instructions to read, ideally using picture cues whenever feasible. The focus should be on the content, not on the complexities of the task. The same holds true for testing very young learners, especially those who lack literacy in their first language.

Although much maligned, the standard objective formats such as MCQ, T/F/NG, and matching have a valuable place in reading assessment if they are carefully constructed. As Alderson (2000, p. 218) notes, these formats can be used in sophisticated ways. One of the keys to effective use is to embed items in rich context whenever possible. After all, in real life we seldom encounter discourse that wildly jumps from one topic to another. Context is especially important if your focus is on grammar or vocabulary since structures and words do not occur in a vacuum. A paragraph that tests structural items or vocabulary is far more valid because the items appear in context. Moreover, in contextualized gap fills, students can attend to the surrounding words to choose appropriate collocations. Here is an example of contextualized multiple choice cloze focusing on certain grammar points such as articles, prepositions, pronouns, verb tense, and agreement. It is an example of a rational deletion where certain words have been omitted in order to test specified points.

Example of Rational Deletion Cloze for Grammar in Context

Read the paragraph, and decide which words from the chart are best for the spaces.

Mark Twain was one of the most popular writers in America. His real name was Samuel Langhorne Clemens, and he was born ① 1835 in the state of Missouri. For most of his life, he ② near the great Mississippi River, ③ when he was thirty, he traveled to California. He became famous the following year when he wrote a short story called "The Celebrated Jumping Frog of Calaveras County." After that, he traveled ④ the world and continued ⑤ writing career. Twain's ⑥ known book was *The Adventures of Huckleberry Finn*, a story of a young boy's life on the Mississippi River. By the 1880s, Twain had become ⑦ important name in U.S. literature. Even today, long after his death, Mark Twain ⑧ famous for his skill at writing the same way people talk.

Circle the word that is best for each space.

space number	choice a	choice b	choice c
1	on	at	in
2	lived	lives	living
3	because	or	but
4	upon	around	into
5	her	his	its
6	better	best	bigger
7	an	the	a
8	was	is	be

Source: Adapted from K. S. Folse, *Intermediate Reading Practices: Building Reading and Vocabulary Skills* (3rd ed.) Ann Arbor: University of Michigan Press, 2004, p. 27.

Multiple Choice Format

A wide variety of reading subskills are tested using MCQs, but the format is well-suited for testing the ability to distinguish between main ideas and supporting details. Reading experts believe that recognizing levels of generality is crucial to comprehending the interrelationship of ideas in a reading text. A standard technique is to have response options correspond to different levels of specificity in these ways:

- **JR** (just right). This option should be the correct or best answer.
- **TG** (too general). This distractor relates to an option that is too broad.
- **TS** (too specific). This distractor focuses on one detail within the text or paragraph.
- **OT** (off topic). Depending on the level of the students, this distractor is written so that it reflects an idea that is <u>not</u> developed in the paragraph or text. For more advanced students, the idea would be related in some way, but does not represent the main idea.

Alternatively, MCQs can be used to directly check on the main idea for a particular section of the text (such as a paragraph) or for the text as a whole, often done through choosing the best title.

As testing boards shift some of their emphasis to comprehension above the sentence level, MCQs are used to assess reference, discourse markers, and insertion points for missing sentences. It is important to check the guidelines for good item writing as tasks become more complex.

True/False/Not Given Format

Initially, T/F/NGs seem easier to write than MCQs with all their pitfalls. However, there are several points to keep in mind. First, you <u>can</u> use the NG option for reading as long as students can refer to the text so you do not test memory. This is standard practice with many standardized exams, including computer versions, where students have access to the text until they have completed the relevant section or time is up.

Second, as previously noted, phrase all statements affirmatively and avoid extremes such as *always* or *never* because they tip off students that the answer is false. Provide answers for students to mark instead of expecting them to write in letters because it is sometimes difficult to tell the difference between a student's T and an F!

Have several texts within any reading assessment to avoid problems that may occur if some students respond poorly to a topic or the associated vocabulary. Practical considerations such as limited time to develop texts sometimes result in using the same passage for different question formats. If you encounter this situation, make sure that your specifications clearly state how each format is to be used so that target skills and items don't overlap. Examine this section of a reading assessment that uses a single text for both MCQ and T/F/NG formats. The following text and questions are based on the earlier specifications and illustrate technical points in writing items for reading assessment.

Example of Two Formats Using One Text

Read the text, and then answer the questions.

Diamonds

They are just tiny pieces of carbon, like coal. However, diamonds are the hardest substances in nature and are extremely valuable. Why are diamonds so special, how did they get here, and why are they worth so much money?

Diamonds are famous for two qualities: their extreme hardness and their brilliance at changing white light into a rainbow of colors. Their strength is important in industry where diamonds are used to cut, drill, engrave, and polish other materials. Their brilliance makes them valuable as gemstones for jewelry.

Diamonds formed billions of years ago in the Earth's mantle, one hundred miles below the surface, under conditions of great pressure and high temperatures. Much later, deep volcanic eruptions brought them to the surface. Magma, very hot liquid rock, carried diamonds to the Earth's surface in pipes, carrot-shaped tubes made up of other kinds of rocks. As the rock approached the Earth's surface, huge explosions occurred. Δ When the pipes cooled, they contained small amounts of diamonds. Usually, diamonds are mined from the pipes, but at other times, people collect them where they have **eroded** into rivers or ocean beaches.

Historical records show that people in India about 2,500 years ago thought diamonds came from the gods. **They** were used in religious ceremonies. Later, diamonds got their name from the Greek word *adamas* which meant invincible or too strong to defeat. The Roman writer Pliny (23–79 CE) noted that diamonds were both beautiful and very useful to **engravers**, people who scratch designs on other hard metals. Then, for about 1,000 years, nobody paid much attention to diamonds.

In the Middle Ages, European and Asian royalty used diamonds in their crowns. French King Louis the Ninth (1214–70) believed that diamonds were so special only kings should have them. Later, though, other wealthy people used diamond jewelry. Up to this point, most diamonds still came from India.

In 1726, diamonds were found in Brazil and a hundred years later, mines in Africa started producing diamonds. Now half of the world's diamonds still come from Africa, but places such as Canada, Siberia, and Australia also produce them. The stone waste surrounding diamonds is about 99 percent, so diamonds are quite rare. About 80 percent of all diamonds are used in industry and only 20 percent become jewelry. The rough gemstone diamonds get cut, polished, and shaped in Antwerp and Amsterdam, New York, Tel Aviv, and in Surat, India. Today, most small diamonds are processed in Surat.

The DeBeers Company controls the production and sales of diamonds throughout the world. In the 1930s, they started an advertising campaign to convince Americans that they should buy diamond engagement rings. The idea caught on, and most couples spend a lot of money on diamond rings. The jewelry is often overpriced to make more profit for the company. Today, there is a concern that some African diamond producers sell stones to buy guns to support warfare and other criminal activities. In 2002, many nations signed the Kimberly Agreement to stop this illegal trade in diamonds.

Source: http://en.wikipedia.org/wiki/Diamond

Part 1: Circle the letter of the best answer.

1. Where did diamonds develop?

    A. billions of years ago

    B. along rivers and beaches

    C. deep in the Earth's mantle

    D. from pressure and high temperatures

2. In the fourth paragraph, what does *they* rcfcr to?

    A. historical records

    B. diamonds

    C. Indian people

    D. the gods

3. An engraver uses diamonds _____.

    A. as a tool to make designs

    B. by creating crowns for kings

    C. to be strong in battles

    D. for religious ceremonies

4. The main idea of the sixth paragraph is _____.

    A. Canada and Siberia are cold places

    B. diamond production and processing

    C. the use of diamonds in industry

    D. 50 percent of diamonds come from Africa

5. Which sentence fits best at the Δ mark in the third paragraph?

    A. You can see these crowns at the Tower of London.

    B. Diamonds are mostly colorless, but some have colors.

    C. These stolen stones are often called conflict diamonds.

    D. The blasts were caused by hot magma hitting water.

Part 2: Decide if the statement is true (T), false (F), or not given (NG), and circle your answer.

T   F   NG   6. The most important quality of diamond jewelry is its extreme hardness.

T   F   NG   7. Industry uses carbon to make valuable diamonds.

T   F   NG   8. Water causes diamonds to move from volcanic tubes to the ocean.

T   F   NG   9. About 80 percent of American women wear diamond engagement rings.

T   F   NG   10. The author thinks that people buy diamond jewelry because of advertising.

Short Answer Format

Scanning for information in charts, tables, or advertisements is a real-life task and lends itself well to the short answer format. As previously discussed, consider the type of task when making decisions about the degree of accuracy expected in terms of spelling, capitalization, etc. All too often, short answer items focus on details, but they can be used to assess other reading skills. For example, students may supply an appropriate title for a chart or diagram to check their grasp of main ideas. If chart, map, or graph reading is important in your program, frame short answer items so students have to demonstrate they understand how these graphics work. For example, what do the axes on a graph represent, what trends can they discern, what information is at the intersection of certain columns and rows? You can also ask for short answers about symbols, sources, and dates of scanned material. This task demonstrates some of these points.

Example of Short Answer Scanning Task

Scan the following chart on the World's Longest Rivers and answer each question with three words or less.

1. Which river is longer than 4,000 miles? _____

2. How many of the longest rivers are in Asia? _____

3. How many rivers start in mountainous areas? _____

4. Which river is really two rivers together? _____

5. Which rivers are not important for shipping? _____

6. Did the information come from the Internet or a book?

   _____

7. Which rivers flow north? _____

8. Which river has the most water in it? _____

The World's Longest Rivers

Name	Continent	Starts in	Ends in	Direction of Flow	Length in Miles	Navigation
Nile	Africa	Lake Victoria	Mediterranean Sea	North	4,180	
Amazon*	South America	Andes Mountains	Atlantic Ocean	East	3,912	
Mississippi (including Missouri River)	North America	Rocky Mountains	Atlantic Ocean	South	3,710	
Yangtze	Asia	Tibet Plateau	Pacific Ocean	East	3,602	
Ob	Asia	Altai Mountains	Arctic Ocean	North	3,459	

* = greatest amount of water flow

= important for shipping

Source: www.adventurelandtravel.com/LargestRivers.htm

Sequencing Tasks

There are many ways to check students' understanding of the organization of a text, but sequencing is especially useful in reading a narrative, following steps in instructions or a recipe, or understanding biographical or historical events. Just as jumbled or jigsaw texts are useful teaching tools, re-ordering sentences or paragraphs can be used for assessment providing that students have already encountered them in classroom instruction. Cognitively, these tasks are closely related to text insertion tasks because they focus on seeing how the parts of a text fit together to form a coherent whole. When you design these tasks, it is important to create logical linkages between each component so that it is clear how they fit together. You can do this by repeating certain key words or names, by chronological sequencing, or by logical connections. It is also good practice to indicate the starting point and "anchor" several other points. Examine this example for some of these techniques.

Example of Sequencing Task

Number the paragraphs in the correct order to make a reading passage about Amelia Earhart's life. Paragraphs 1, 5, and 7 are done for you.

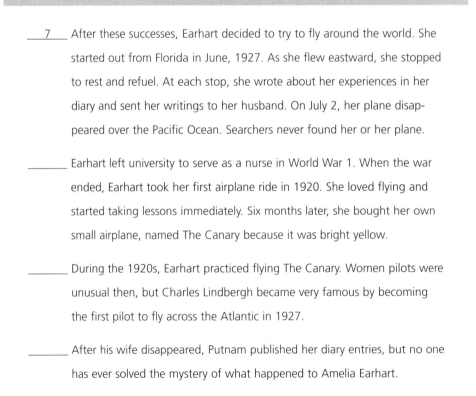

    7   After these successes, Earhart decided to try to fly around the world. She started out from Florida in June, 1927. As she flew eastward, she stopped to rest and refuel. At each stop, she wrote about her experiences in her diary and sent her writings to her husband. On July 2, her plane disappeared over the Pacific Ocean. Searchers never found her or her plane.

           Earhart left university to serve as a nurse in World War 1. When the war ended, Earhart took her first airplane ride in 1920. She loved flying and started taking lessons immediately. Six months later, she bought her own small airplane, named The Canary because it was bright yellow.

           During the 1920s, Earhart practiced flying The Canary. Women pilots were unusual then, but Charles Lindbergh became very famous by becoming the first pilot to fly across the Atlantic in 1927.

           After his wife disappeared, Putnam published her diary entries, but no one has ever solved the mystery of what happened to Amelia Earhart.

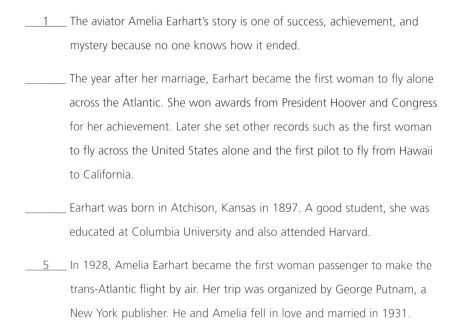

___1___ The aviator Amelia Earhart's story is one of success, achievement, and
mystery because no one knows how it ended.

_____ The year after her marriage, Earhart became the first woman to fly alone
across the Atlantic. She won awards from President Hoover and Congress
for her achievement. Later she set other records such as the first woman
to fly across the United States alone and the first pilot to fly from Hawaii
to California.

_____ Earhart was born in Atchison, Kansas in 1897. A good student, she was
educated at Columbia University and also attended Harvard.

___5___ In 1928, Amelia Earhart became the first woman passenger to make the
trans-Atlantic flight by air. Her trip was organized by George Putnam, a
New York publisher. He and Amelia fell in love and married in 1931.

Combination Tasks

Some tasks combine formats for particular purposes. Earlier, we saw a gap-fill
task used to assess grammar in context. In that case, students had to select the
appropriate supplied answer. Sometimes, however, we want to have students
produce quite a bit of language to demonstrate their understanding of both the
meaning and the structure of the reading passage. Some testers favor fixed-ratio
cloze for this, a format where every seventh word is deleted. Others go further
with C-tests in which half of every other word is missing.

There is, however, a middle-ground possibility where students supply key
terms as a cloze summary of a long text or demonstrate their understanding of
details from a graphic. The following example uses a model that is common in
the social sciences, one that appears in many first-year university courses in
sociology or geography. Each gap requires the student to demonstrate understanding of how the model works. In this case, it is possible for students to use
several different words with similar meanings such as decline, drop, or
decrease, and the teacher would have to consider them equally correct.
Another approach is to supply the words in a base form in alphabetical order
with several logical distractors included.

Example of Information Transfer from Graphic to Gapped Text

Read the diagram of the Demographic Transition and then complete the text with appropriate words.

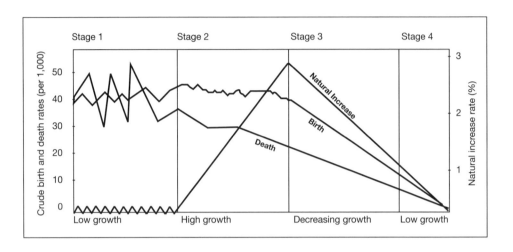

The demographic transition is a model that social scientists use to explain how populations change over time. The model has four **1.**_____ or sections. Each one shows a different situation with birth and **2.**_____ rates that results in a particular pattern of natural **3.**_____.

In the first stage, both birth and death rates are relatively high, but they cancel each other out so that the result is **4.**_____ growth. This is enough for the population to continue, but it does not **5.**_____.

In the next stage, birth rates continue to be relatively **6.**_____, but death rates start to **7.**_____. In developing societies, this has happened as the result of better **8.**_____ care, nutrition and **9.**_____ to fight disease. Overall, more people survive, resulting in a **10.**_____ rate of **11.**_____ increase.

In the third stage, **12.**_____ birth and death rates **13.**_____, so the rate of natural increase **14.**_____ declines. At the beginning of the third stage it is still **15.**_____, but by the end of the stage, people have **16.**_____

children and the rate drops. However, there are still more **17.**_____ than

18._____, so there is a **19.**_____ rate of natural increase.

The final or fourth stage is characterized by **20.**_____ birth and death rates.
As birth rates **21.**_____ to the **22.**_____ of death rates, the rate of
23._____ **24.**_____ also falls. In fact, it can **25.**_____ to below the
rate of replacement of the population. Some contemporary societies that have
reached this point are concerned about what their population levels will be in a
few decades.

Given the importance of reading for general and academic purposes, a variety of assessment techniques is available to teachers, yet we have only sampled some of the most common ones. In thinking about reading assessment for your class, be sure to check what skills, techniques, and formats are used on standardized tests that your students must take. Analyze publicly available material (i.e., official released items), and then try writing practice tests. As your students use them, discuss how they work and what they are testing. You will be developing good reading as well as test-taking skills.

Ten Things to Remember about Reading Assessment

1. **Make sure your assessment matches your reading program.**
   Test the skills you teach, and consider the target situation of your learners when developing reading assessment.

2. **Sample a range of reading subskills with different task types.**
   Variety is good, but use four to ten items for each task type to avoid students' scores being affected by constant adjustment to different tasks.

3. **Choose a range of text types appropriate to your program.**
   Consider students' background knowledge and interests in selecting texts. Some familiarity with the topic or vocabulary aids comprehension. However, students should actually have to read the text and not simply rely on prior knowledge in responding to questions. Never use texts that students have already read!

4. **Use both prose and non-linear texts.**
   Don't forget that many daily reading tasks use non-linear texts such as diagrams, graphs, maps, and schedules. If you teach students to read non-linear texts, then by all means include them in assessment. <u>Remember</u>: Good assessment mirrors actual teaching.

5. **Use authentic or adapted texts whenever possible.**
   Check the texts for readability levels and vocabulary. Be certain that copied authentic materials are legible! Credit your sources.

6. **Exploit the entire text.**
   Vary whole-text questions with those that focus on specific sections. Questions should cover all sections of a text.

7. **Include grammar and vocabulary in context.**
   Emphasize the importance of structure and vocabulary to reading comprehension by including these contributing skills in your assessment.

8. **There is a place for separate assessment of grammar and vocabulary.**
   Sometimes you will want to focus classroom assessment on recently covered grammar points or vocabulary.

9. **Assess inferencing and critical thinking.**
   It is easy to ask questions about specific, stated details, but much more challenging to create items that require students to think beyond the printed text. Include questions that require students to think beyond what they see in print.

10. **Consider timing to assess skimming and scanning.**
    Since these reading strategies need to be performed quickly, think about their placement in your assessment. If you cannot time separate sections, place scanning tasks at the end.

Extension Activity

Mr. Knott uses reading texts from the news because he wants to make his students more aware of current events. He gave this reading test to his ninth grade classes. See if you can identify some areas for improvement.

Mr. Knott's Reading Test

Grade 9 Reading Test

Name: _____ Date: _____ Class: _____

Read the passage and answer the questions.

Alligators are part of nature in Florida, but when three women die from alligator attacks in one week, people become worried. Florida has about two million alligators and for 58 years until now, there have only been 17 fatal attacks on humans. Why are there suddenly more fatal alligator attacks?

Wildlife experts say that we can learn from looking at the three recent attacks and understanding more about the habits of alligators. Alligators can grow to 14 feet long, and they can move very quickly, up to 30 miles per hour. They prefer fresh water with lots of plants in it, and they are most active from sunset to sunrise. The three deaths happened in different parts of the state, but they have some things in common. Two of the recent deaths occurred when women were walking or sitting near a canal, something like a man-made river that carries fresh water from one place to another. It is believed that they weren't paying close attention to things around them. The third woman died when she was snorkeling in a lake in Ocala National Forest late in the afternoon. Perhaps the women didn't realize how strong alligators are and how fast they can move when they are hungry.

Years ago, laws were passed to protect alligators, but now authorities such as police and wildlife managers get more than 18,000 telephone calls a year about "nuisance alligators" that cause problems. Wildlife officers can trap and kill problem animals more than four feet long. They say that it is harder for people and alligators to co-exist or live together nowadays. For one thing, Florida is a popular place to live because of its warm climate, and people like to live near the water. Some residents like to keep alligators as pets or feed them so they can take photographs close-up. They even pick them up and touch them. This is dangerous and against the law. Other people are careless and don't watch young children or pet dogs near the water. They should never be left alone near the water.

Other authorities give two natural reasons for the attacks in May. First, the dry weather this year has created very low water levels and alligators travel to find deeper water. That means they are in canals, swimming pools, and golf course ponds where people do not expect to find them. Secondly, alligators mate in the warm months. The males are most active from April to June, and then the females protect their babies from June to August. Wildlife experts say people have to think about all these things to prevent more alligator attacks.

1. What word in Paragraph 2 means "water like a river"?

   _____

2. How many people have died from alligator attacks?
   A. 58
   B. 14
   C. 17
   D. 20

Write T (true), F (false), or DK (don't know) next to the statements.

3. _____ Alligators are most active during the day.

4. _____ You can run away because alligators cannot move quickly.

5. _____ The weather this year has been wetter than usual.

6. _____ It's okay to feed your pet alligator.

7. In the third paragraph, what does *they* refer to?
   A. pet dogs
   B. young children
   C. residents
   D. police

8. Which place are you <u>least</u> likely to find alligators?
   A. swimming pools
   B. the ocean
   C. canals
   D. golf course ponds

9. What does *co-exist* mean? _____

10. Which is the best title for this reading?
    A. Alligator Behavior
    B. Alligator Attacks
    C. Ocala National Forest
    D. Wildlife Protection

Critical Thinking Section

Put a check (✓) next to all the things that help prevent alligator attacks.

_____ Swim during the day in salt water or swimming pools.

_____ Let your children play near the water alone.

_____ Feed alligators if they come near your house.

_____ Take photographs of alligators from a distance only.

_____ Beware of alligators during their mating season.

_____ Call the police about "nuisance alligators."

_____ Sit and relax by canals with your feet in the water.

Which sentence means the same thing as, "Wildlife officers can trap and kill problem animals over 4 feet long"?

1. Wildlife officers enjoy killing large alligators.
2. Authorities protect young alligators under four feet in length.
3. Traps are too small for large alligators.
4. It is too difficult to locate small alligators underwater.

Ms. Wright's Comments on Mr. Knott's Reading Test

First, while I applaud Mr. Knott's attempt to make his students more aware of current events, he needs to be more selective about the topic. A text about alligator attacks is certain to raise some anxiety among students in Florida! No doubt Mr. Knott intended to provide a public safety message, but this text would have been more appropriate for a class discussion where students could be reassured about the actual dangers.

That said, I'd like to commend Mr. Knott for attempting to assess a wide range of reading subskills and not just focus on specific details, which is so often the case. He evenly uses most sections of the text and asks questions about both grammar and vocabulary in context. I appreciate his focus on critical thinking, both in the labeled section and in other questions based on inferencing skills. However, I wonder if it is advisable to label these as something special? Ideally, <u>all</u> questions would utilize critical thinking.

My main concerns have to do with test and item construction. Although Mr. Knott did follow the specifications with regard to subskills to be covered, the organization of his test is quite chaotic. In a reading or listening exam, it is important to stick to one format for subsections of the exam so that students don't constantly have to adjust to task changes. Within each subsection, the questions should occur in the same order as the content of the passage. Next time, Mr. Knott should mark up the text so he can clearly see the progression of testable points.

There are also technical problems with his test. There is no clear indication of how many points each question or section is worth. Some sections have instructions while others don't. Even those with instructions have problems. For example, what does Mr. Knott intend by "DK—don't know"? Perhaps he has confused it with "NG," meaning that information is not given in the passage. On the other hand, maybe he means that the question is unanswerable by the student. Item 4 in that section is especially problematic because of the implied double negative with "cannot" and a negative response. Mr. Knott could also be more consistent with the formatting of his MCQs.

In several places there are problems with keys, the intended answers. In question 2, either 17 or 20 would be correct since he doesn't specify the time frame. In question 7, all of the answers are plausible since it is not clear which they he intends to reference in paragraph 3. Paraphrasing is an important reading skill, and it is good that Mr. Knott chose to test it. However, in item 2, will students understand the meaning of "fatal" in the text and relate it to "died"? In item 8, will they understand "least"? In addition, some distractors could be eliminated without students even reading the text. Lastly, Mr. Knott forgot to credit his sources.

4 Assessing Writing

How important is writing in your school's assessment of your learners?		
(A) **Intensive English Program, Community College, University (-Bound) Program:** Writing is fundamental to academic success and is certainly a major component of any type of assessment. Many post-secondary programs require a writing sample before admission. The TOEFL requires several writing samples from students.	(B) **Conversation Classes, Non-academic Programs, Survival Classes:** Writing is not important and is rarely tested. However, learners may need a certain level of writing ability for certain short answer or short essay questions.	(C) **K-12:** Along with reading, writing is considered one of the most important academic skills that all students are expected to master. Test scorers need to realize that a certain number of language errors will persist for some time with ELLs, namely errors with articles, prepositions, and verb tenses. These errors are peculiar to ELLs and should not be graded as harshly as material that was taught to everyone such as spelling or punctuation. Teachers should be aware of the importance of a clear, easy-to-understand, culturally-neutral prompt for the exam. Content area teachers from science and social studies should realize that any essay question will almost always produce a lower score from ELLs because of their language problems even when they know the content material well.

The field of writing assessment has developed considerably over the past 50 years. Teachers ask their students to write on a variety of topics and then assess them on the message contained in the writing sample, the clarity and organization of the message, and the mechanics (spelling, capitalization, and punctuation) utilized (O'Malley & Valdez Pierce, 1996). This chapter explores the practical issues that teachers face when evaluating the writing work of their students.

Assessing writing skills is important because good writing ability is highly sought by higher education institutions and employers. To this end, Ms. Wright spends a lot of time ensuring that her writing assessment practices are valid and reliable. She knows that any type of assessment should reflect the course goals, so she starts the test development process by reviewing the course outcomes and the specifications. Some of the things she does to ensure valid and reliable writing assessment are:

- She avoids a "snapshot" approach of assessing writing ability by giving students plenty of opportunities to practice a variety of writing skills.
- She practices multiple-measures writing assessment by using tasks that focus both on product (midterm and final essays) and process (writing portfolio).
- She gives frequent writing assessments because she knows that assessment is more reliable when there are more samples to assess.
- She doesn't give students a choice of writing topic on important exams like midterm and final because the marking will be more difficult to standardize if she does.
- She avoids using a red pen to mark her students' papers as she feels it does more harm than good. When papers are submitted electronically, she uses computerized marking programs.
- Before marking begins, she identifies benchmark papers and later shows them to students during instruction.
- She uses a well-established analytic marking scale at midterm because several inexperienced teachers will be helping grade papers.
- She makes sure that at least two teachers mark every writing test.

Approaches to Writing Assessment

Two major approaches to writing assessment have been identified in the literature—indirect and direct.

Indirect measures of writing assessment assess correct usage in sentence-level constructions and assess spelling and punctuation via objective formats like multiple choice and cloze tests. These measures are supposed to determine a student's knowledge of writing sub-skills such as grammar and sentence construction, which are assumed to constitute components of writing ability. Indirect writing assessment measures are more concerned with accuracy than communication. In the past, tests such as TOEFL® used indirect writing assessment where four sections of a sentence were underlined and marked as "A," "B," "C," and "D." One of these contained an error, and students had to identify the error.

Direct measures of writing assessment assess a student's ability to communicate through the written mode based on the actual production of written texts. This type of writing assessment requires the student to produce the content; find a way to organize the ideas; and use appropriate vocabulary, grammatical conventions, and syntax. Direct writing assessment integrates all elements of writing.

Considerations in Designing Writing Assessment Tasks

According to Hyland (2003), the design of good writing assessment tests and tasks involves four basic elements:

- *Rubric:* the instructions
- *Prompt:* the task
- *Expected response:* what the teacher intends students to do with the task
- *Post-task evaluation:* assessing the effectiveness of the writing task.

The first element of a good writing assessment is the *rubric,* the instructions for carrying out the writing task. A rubric can also mean the set of criteria on which a piece of work, such as a project, is evaluated, and it is used in this sense in elementary education. Good writing instructions or rubrics should:

- specify a particular rhetorical pattern, length of writing desired, and amount of time allowed to complete the task
- indicate the resources students will have available at their disposal (dictionaries, spell/grammar checker, etc.), and the delivery method of the assessment (i.e., paper and pencil, laptop, PC)
- indicate whether a draft or an outline is required
- include the overall weighting of the writing task as compared to other parts of the exam

Most of the information in the rubric should come from the *test specification*. Test specifications for a writing test should provide the test writer with details on the range of topics, the rhetorical pattern to be tested, the intended audience, how much information should be included in the rubric, the number of words the student is expected to produce, and overall weighting (Davidson & Lloyd, 2005). Here is an example related to an essay on travel.

Sample Writing Test Specification

Topic	Related to the theme of travel
Text Type	Compare/contrast
Length	250 words
Areas to be assessed	Content, organization, vocabulary, language use, mechanics
Timing	30 minutes
Weighting	10 percent of midterm exam grade
Pass level	Similar to IELTS™ band 5.5

The second essential part of any test of writing is the *writing prompt*. Hyland (2003) defines the prompt as "the stimulus the student must respond to" (p. 221). Kroll and Reid (1994) identify three main prompt formats: base, framed, and text-based (p. 233). The first two are the most common in second/foreign language writing assessment. Base prompts state the entire task in direct and simple terms, whereas framed prompts present the writer with a situation that acts as a frame for the interpretation of the task. Text-based prompts present writers with a text to which they must respond or utilize in their writing. Consider these examples.

Base Prompts

- Do you favor or oppose a complete ban on smoking? Why? Why not?
- Discuss the view that women are better drivers than men.
- Many say that "Money is the root of all evil." Do you agree or disagree with this statement?

Framed Prompts

- On a recent flight back home to the UAE, Emirates Airlines lost your baggage. Write a complaint letter to Mr. Al-Ahli, the General Manager, telling him about your problem. Be sure to include the following:
  —your flight details
  —a description of the baggage lost and its contents
  —what you would like Mr. Al-Ahli to do for you
- An announcement has been made by the Academy on this year's nominations for the Oscar awards. You and most of your friends have not heard of the films nominated for the Best Picture award. Write a letter to the head of the Academy Awards about this, and suggest and support alternative nominees.

Text-Based Prompts

- You have been asked by a youth travel magazine to write an article about things to see and do in your hometown. Using the attached set of pictures, write a one-page article on this topic.
- You have been put in charge of selecting an appropriate restaurant for your senior class party. Use the restaurant reviews to select an appropriate venue, and then write an invitation letter to your fellow classmates persuading them to join you there.

Criteria of Good Writing Prompts

Each prompt you use in the assessment of writing should meet the following criteria:

- generate the desired type of writing, genre, or rhetorical pattern
- get students involved in thinking and problem-solving
- be accessible, interesting, and challenging to students
- address topics that are meaningful, relevant, and motivating
- not require specialist background knowledge
- use appropriate signpost verbs
- be fair and provide equal opportunities for all students to respond
- be clear, authentic, focused, and unambiguous
- specify an audience, a purpose, and a context

Source: Davidson, P., & Lloyd, D. (2005). Guidelines for developing a reading test. In D. Lloyd, P. Davidson, & C. Coombe (Eds.), *The fundamentals of language assessment: A practical guide for teachers in the Gulf* (pp. 53–63). Dubai: TESOL Arabia Publications.

Developing a good writing prompt requires that you use the appropriate signpost term to match the rhetorical pattern you are using. Some of the most common signpost terms are:

Describe:	give a detailed account
Discuss:	argue a thesis, identifying pros and cons
Explain:	state and interpret
Compare:	show similarities between two things
Contrast:	show the differences between two things
Analyze:	identify main points and evaluate them
Define:	provide the definition and exemplify
Summarize:	produce a concise account of the main ideas, omitting details and examples
Outline:	provide a summary of main points and sub-headings
Evaluate:	appraise the worth or value of something

A third essential element of good writing assessment is the *expected response,* a description of what the teacher intends students to do with the writing task. Before communicating information on the expected response to students, the teacher must have a clear picture of the type of response the assessment task should generate.

Finally, whatever way you choose to assess writing, *evaluate the effectiveness* of your writing tasks/tests. According to Hyland (2003), good writing tasks are likely to produce positive responses to the following questions:

- Did the prompt discriminate well among my students?
- Were the essays easy to read and evaluate?
- Were students able to write to their potential and show what they knew?

Issues in Writing Assessment

Time Allocation

Teachers often ask how much time students should be given to complete writing tasks. Although timing would depend on whether you are assessing process or product, a good rule of thumb is provided by Jacobs, Zinkgraf, Wormuth, Hartfiel, & Hughey, et al. (1981). In their research on the Michigan Composition Test, they state that allowing 30 minutes is probably sufficient time for most students to produce an adequate sample of writing (p. 19). With process-oriented writing or portfolios, much more time should be allocated for assessment tasks.

Process versus Product

In recent years, there has been a shift toward the process of writing rather than on the written product. Some writing tests assess the whole writing process, from brainstorming activities to the final draft or finished product. In using this process approach, students usually have to submit their work in a portfolio that includes all draft material. A more traditional way to assess writing is through a product approach. This is usually accomplished through a timed essay at the middle and end-point of the semester. It is recommended that teachers use a combination of the two approaches in their writing assessment, but the approach ultimately depends on the course objectives.

Use of Technology

Technology has the potential to affect writing assessment. Students writing on computers regularly use spell and grammar checker, a thesaurus, or online dictionaries as tools.

As writing assessment increasingly takes place electronically, access to these tools becomes an issue. If students using computers have access to spell and grammar checkers, does this put those who write by hand at a distinct disadvantage? The issue of skill contamination must also be considered as electronic writing assessment is also a test of keyboarding and computer skills. Whatever delivery mode you use for your writing assessments, it is important to be consistent with all students.

Topic Restriction

Topic restriction, the belief that all students should be asked to write on the same topic with no alternatives allowed, is a controversial issue in writing assessment. Some teachers believe that students perform better when they have the opportunity to select the prompt from a variety of alternatives. When given a choice, students often select a topic that interests them and one for which they have background knowledge. The obvious benefit of providing students with a list of alternatives is that if they do not understand a particular prompt, they will be able to select another, thus reducing student anxiety.

On the other hand, the major disadvantage of providing more than one prompt is that it is difficult to write prompts that are at the same level of difficulty, thus creating variance in scores. Moreover, marker consistency may be reduced if all papers read at a single writing calibration session are not on the same topic. It is the consensus within the language testing community that all students should write on the same topic and preferably on more than one topic. However, research results are mixed on whether students write better with single or multiple prompts (Hamp-Lyons, 1990b). It is thought that the performance of students who are given multiple prompts may be lower than expected because students often waste time selecting a topic instead of writing. If you decide to allow students to select a topic from a variety of alternatives, make sure your alternative topics are the same genre and rhetorical pattern. This practice will make it easier for you to achieve inter-rater reliability.

Techniques for Assessing Writing

The ESL/EFL literature generally addresses two types of writing—free writing and guided writing. Free writing requires students to read a prompt that poses a situation and write a planned response based on a combination of background knowledge and knowledge learned from the course. Guided writing, in contrast, requires students to manipulate content that is provided in the prompt, usually in the form of a chart or diagram.

Guided Writing

Guided writing is a bridge between objective and subjective formats. This task requires teachers to be clear about what they expect students to do. Decide in advance whether mechanical issues such as spelling, punctuation, and capitalization matter when the task focuses on comprehension. Some important points to keep in mind for guided writing are:

- Be clear about the expected form and length of response (e.g., one paragraph, a 250 word essay, a letter).
- If you want particular information included, clearly specify it in the prompt (e.g., three causes and effects, two supporting details).
- Similarly, specify the discourse pattern(s) the students are expected to use (e.g., compare and contrast, cause and effect, description).
- Since guided writing depends on the students' manipulation of the information provided, ask them to provide something beyond the prompt such as an opinion, an inference, or a prediction.
- Be amenable to revising the anticipated answer even as you grade.

Free-Writing

All of these suggestions are particularly germane to free-writing. The goal for teachers is to elicit comparable products from students of different ability levels. Some important points to keep in mind for free-writing are:

- The use of multiple raters is especially important in evaluating free-writing. Agree on grading criteria in advance and calibrate before the actual grading session.
- Decide whether to use holistic, analytical, or a combination of the two as a rating scale for marking.
- If using a band or rating scale (see pages 82–83 for an example), adjust it to the task.
- Acquaint students with the marking scheme in advance by using it for teaching, grading homework and providing feedback. (<u>Remember</u>: in all cases, good assessment mirrors actual classroom instruction.)

- Teach good writing strategies by providing students with enough space for an outline, a draft, and the finished product.
- In ESL/EFL classrooms, be aware of cultural differences and sensitivities. Avoid contentious issues that might offend or disadvantage students.

Authentic Writing Assessment

Student-Teacher Conferences

Teachers can learn a lot about their students' writing habits through student-teacher conferences, which can also provide important assessment opportunities. The questions teachers might ask during conferences include:

- How did you select this topic?
- What did you do to generate content for this writing?
- Before you started writing, did you make a plan or an outline?
- During the editing phase, what types of errors did you find in your writing?
- What do you feel are your strengths in writing?
- What do you find difficult in writing?
- What would you like to improve about your writing?

Self-Assessment

Two self-assessment techniques can be used in writing assessment—dialogue journals and learning logs. *Dialogue journals* require students to regularly make entries addressed to the teacher on topics of their choice. The teacher writes back, modeling appropriate language use but not correcting the students' language. Dialogue journals can be in a paper/pencil or electronic format. Students typically write in class for a five- to ten-minute period at the beginning or end of the class. If you want to use dialogue journals in your classes, don't assess students on language accuracy. Instead, Peyton and Reed (1990) recommend that you assess students on areas like topic initiation, elaboration, variety, use of different genres, expressions of interests and attitudes, and awareness about the writing process. *Learning logs* document time students spend on various writing activities.

Peer Assessment

Peer assessment, yet another assessment technique, involves the students in the evaluation of writing. One advantage of peer assessment is that it eases the marking burden on the teacher. Teachers do not need to mark every single piece of student writing, but it is important that students receive regular feedback on what they produce. Students can use checklists, scoring rubrics, or simple questions for peer assessment. The major rationale for peer assessment is that when students learn to evaluate the work of their peers, they are extending their own learning opportunities.

Portfolio-Based Assessment

Portfolio-based assessment examines multiple pieces of writing produced over time under different constraints rather than a single essay written in a specified time period. For assessment purposes, a portfolio is a collection of student writing over time that shows the stages in the writing process a text has gone through and thus the stages of the writers' growth. Portfolios reflect accomplishment relative to specific instructional goals or objectives. Portfolios can showcase a student's best work or display a collection of both drafts and final products to demonstrate progress and continued improvement.

Characteristics of a Portfolio

Several well-known testers have put forth lists of characteristics that exemplify good portfolios. For instance, Paulson, Paulson, and Meyer (1991) believe that portfolios must include student participation in four important areas: (1) the selection of portfolio contents, (2) the guidelines for selection, (3) the criteria for judging merit, and (4) evidence of student reflection.

By including reflection as part of the portfolio process, students are asked to think about their needs, goals, weaknesses, and strengths in language learning. They are also asked to select their best work and explain why it was beneficial to them. Learner reflection allows students to contribute their own insights about their learning to the assessment process. Santos (1997) says it best: "without reflection, the portfolio remains 'a folder of all my papers.'"

Marking Procedures for the Assessment of Writing

Reliable writing assessment requires a carefully thought-out set of procedures, and a significant amount of time needs to be devoted to the rating process.

First, a small team of trained and experienced raters needs to select a number of sample benchmark scripts or papers from completed exam papers. These benchmark papers need to be representative of the following levels at minimum:

- Clear pass (good piece of writing that is solidly in the A/B range)
- Borderline pass (a paper that is on the borderline between pass and fail but shows enough of the requisite information to be a pass)
- Borderline fail (a paper that is on the borderline between pass and fail but does not have enough of the requisite information to pass)
- Clear fail (a below-average paper that is clearly in the D/F range)

Once benchmark papers have been selected, a team of experienced raters marks the papers using the scoring criteria and agrees on a score. It will be helpful to note a few of the reasons why the paper was rated as it was. Next, the lead arbitrator conducts a calibration session (often referred to as a standardization or norming session) where the entire pool of raters rate the sample papers and try to agree on the scores that each paper should receive. In calibration sessions, teachers should evaluate and discuss benchmark papers until they arrive at a consensus score. These sessions are time consuming and not popular with teachers who want to get started marking right away. Sessions can also get heated, especially when raters of different educational and cultural backgrounds are involved. Despite these disadvantages, they are an essential component to standardizing writing scores.

Writing Assessment Scales

An important part of writing assessment deals with selecting the appropriate writing scale for a particular teaching context. Factors to consider include the availability of resources, amount of time allocated to getting reliable writing marks to administration, the teacher population, and the management structure of the institution.

The two main types of writing scales for assessing student written proficiency are holistic and analytic.

Holistic Marking Scales

Holistic marking is based on the marker's total impression of the essay as a whole. Holistic marking is variously termed as impressionistic, global, or integrative marking. Experts in holistic marking scales believe that this type of marking is quick and reliable if three to four people mark each paper. The rule of thumb for holistic marking is to mark for two hours and then take a rest, grading no more than 20 papers per hour. Holistic marking is most successful using scales of a limited range (e.g., from 0–6).

Both the Educational Testing Service (ETS) and the International English Language Testing Systems (IELTS™) have conducted a tremendous amount of research in the area of holistic marking, and second and foreign language educators have identified a number of advantages to it. First, it is reliable if done under no time constraints and if teachers receive adequate training. Second, this type of marking is generally perceived to be quicker than other types of writing assessment and enables a large number of scripts to be scored in a short period of time. Third, since overall writing ability is assessed, students are not disadvantaged by one lower component such as poor grammar bringing down a score. Finally, the scores tend to emphasize the writer's strengths (Cohen, 1994, p. 315).

Several disadvantages of holistic marking have also been identified. First, it can be unreliable if marking is done under short time constraints and with inexperienced, untrained teachers (Heaton, 1990). Second, Cohen (1994) has cautioned that longer essays often tend to receive higher marks. Third, testers point out that reducing a score to one figure tends to reduce the reliability of the overall mark. It is also difficult to interpret a composite score from a holistic mark. The most serious problem associated with holistic marking is its inability to provide washback. Specifically, when marks are assigned through a holistic marking scale, there is no diagnostic information on how they were awarded. Thus, testers often find it difficult to justify the rationale for the mark. Hamp-Lyons (1990a) has stated that holistic marking is severely limited in that it does not provide a profile of the student's writing ability. Finally, since this type of scale looks at writing as a whole, there is the tendency on the part of the marker to overlook the various sub-skills that make up writing.

See Figure 2 on page 82 for an example of a holistic marking scale produced by the National Admissions and Placement Office in the United Arab Emirates for the Common Educational Proficiency Assessment (CEPA).

Figure 2. CEPA Writing Descriptors

6	• Overall meaning of complex communication adequately conveyed.
	• Main and subsidiary points are clear and well organized, but may contain minor irrelevancies or inappropriacies.
	• A range of cohesive devices used, though not always accurately.
	• Generally accurate use of sentence structure, though range of complex sentences is limited.
	• Vocabulary choice generally adequate, but may be inadequate to express a wide range of ideas with precision.
	• Most of the time, appropriate choice of words, idioms and register gives the text a feeling of fluency.
	• Occasional errors in spelling may still occur.
	• Uses capital letters, periods, commas, apostrophes, parentheses, and bullets, with only occasional unobtrusive errors.
5	• Overall meaning of simple and more complex communication adequately conveyed, though clarity will vary.
	• Organization of text contributes to overall clarity.
	• Range of cohesive devices is attempted.
	• Simple sentences are generally correct; some complex sentences may be used, but not often accurately.
	• Errors in subject-verb agreement may still occur.
	• Vocabulary generally appropriate.
	• Appropriate choice of words, idioms and register occasionally gives glimpses of fluency.
	• Spelling errors still intrude but do not impair meaning.
	• Uses capital letters, periods, commas, and apostrophes appropriately, with only occasional errors.
4	• Meaning clear in straightforward communications; where content is more complex, meaning comes through only intermittently.
	• Simple cohesive devices used appropriately.
	• Can construct simple sentences but errors in subject-verb agreement and word order are frequent.
	• Appropriate choice of basic tenses.
	• Range of vocabulary becomes wider, but may be inappropriate.
	• Text is stilted.
	• Spelling errors intrude though words are mainly recognizable with effort.
	• Uses capital letters and periods almost without error; commas and apostrophes missing or misused.
3	• Meaning only clear in short, simple communications; becomes unclear if content becomes more complex.
	• Little or no evidence of cohesive devices.
	• Attempts simple sentences with some awareness of, but limited control of, basic sentence structure and word order.
	• Vocabulary limited to simplest personal or work-related topics.
	• Spelling of familiar words is generally accurate, but unfamiliar words may be unrecognizable.
	• Uses capital letters and periods most of the time.

2	• Can convey only the simplest ideas. • Begins to produce a few short sentences and phrases independently, but with little or no control of sentence structure. • Vocabulary limited to common words. • Can spell a few common words accurately. • Some evidence of punctuation, but usually inaccurate. • Can copy sentences accurately. • Can write legibly.
1	• Can convey information by positioning words correctly (e.g., name, title). • Essentially unable to make sentences or multi-word messages. • Can write words from memory in a limited range (e.g., name, address, job). • Can form letters accurately and independently, but confuses upper and lower case except when copying. • Can copy words accurately but cannot spell words not given. • Text is so short that only evidence of letter formation or word copying can be assessed.
0	Any of the following • No sample available. • Whole text appears to be copied or memorized and bears no relation to the topic. • Illegible.

Analytical Marking Scales

In analytic marking, "raters provide separate assessments for each of a number of aspects of performance" (Hamp-Lyons, 1991). Scorers mark selected aspects of a piece of writing and assign point values to quantifiable criteria. Analytic marking scales are generally more effective with inexperienced teachers and more reliable for scales with a larger point range.

A number of advantages have been identified with analytic marking. First, unlike holistic marking scales, analytical writing scales provide teachers with a "profile" of their students' strengths and weaknesses in writing, which is very useful for diagnostic feedback. Second, analytic marking is very reliable if done with a population of inexperienced teachers who have had little training and who grade under short time constraints (Heaton, 1990). Finally, training raters is easier because the scales are explicit and detailed.

Just as there are advantages to analytic marking, educators point out a number of disadvantages associated with it. Analytic marking is perceived to be more time consuming because it requires teachers to rate various aspects of a student's essay. It also necessitates a set of specific criteria to be written and scorers to be trained in frequent calibration sessions to ensure that inter-marker differences are reduced to increase validity. Also, teachers tend to focus on specific areas in an essay such as content, organization, grammar, mechanics, and vocabulary. Consequently, analytic marks are often lower than holistically marked papers.

The best-known analytic writing scale is the ESL Composition Profile (Jacobs et al., 1981). This scale contains five component skills, each focusing on an important aspect of composition and weighted according to its approximate importance: content (30 points), organization (20 points), vocabulary (20 points), language use (25 points), and mechanics (5 points). The total weight for each component is further broken into numerical ranges that correspond to four levels from very poor to very good to excellent.

Classroom Teacher as Rater

Should classroom teachers mark their own students' papers? Experts disagree here. Those who are against this warn there is the possibility that teachers might show bias for or against a particular student. Other experts believe the classroom teacher knows the student best and should be included as a marker. Double-blind marking is the recommended ideal with no identifying student information on the scripts.

Multiple Raters

Do we really need more than one marker for student writing samples? The answer is an unequivocal yes. All reputable writing assessment programs use more than one rater to judge essays. In fact, the recommended number is two, with a third in case of extreme disagreement or discrepancy. It is believed that multiple judgments lead to a final score that is closer to a "true" score than any single judgment (Hamp-Lyons, 1990b, p. 79).

Responding to Student Writing

Another essential aspect of marking is providing written feedback to students so they can learn and make improvements to their writing. Probably the most common type of written teacher feedback is handwritten comments at the end or in the margins of the students' papers. Some teachers like to use simple correction codes to provide formative feedback. These codes facilitate marking and minimize the amount of "red" ink on student writings. An example of a common correction code used by teachers follows. Advances in technology provide us with another way of responding to student writing. Electronic feedback is particularly valuable because it can give a combination of handwritten comments and correction codes. Teachers can easily provide commentary and insert corrections through Microsoft Word's track changes function and through simple-to-use software programs like Markin *(www.cict.co.uk/software/markin/)*.

Sample Marking Codes for Writing

sp	Spelling
vt	Verb tense
ww	Wrong word
wv	Wrong verb
☺	Nice idea/content!
⊓	Switch placement
¶	New paragraph
?	I don't understand

Research indicates that teacher written feedback is highly valued by second language writers (F. Hyland, 1998, as cited in Hyland, 2003; Ferris, 2002, p. 135), and many students particularly value feedback on their grammar (Leki, 1990). Although positive remarks are motivating and highly valued by students, Hyland (2003) points out that too much praise or positive commentary early on in a writer's development can make students complacent and discourage revision (p. 187).

Ten Things to Remember about Writing Assessment

1. **Give students multiple writing assessment opportunities.**
   Provide plenty of opportunities for students at all levels to practice the type of writing that you expect them to do on the writing test. Often teachers avoid writing until exam time because it is a lot of work to individually mark several drafts of the same essay.

2. **Test a variety of writing skills and create tasks of varying lengths.**
   Take more than one sample of students' writing. This reduces the variation in performance that might occur from task to task. It is widely believed that the performance on one task is not representative of students' overall writing ability. The more samples of writing ability on the test, the more reliable the test.

3. **Develop prompts that are appropriate for the students.**
   The prompts you select or develop should invite the desired type of writing. They should be realistic and sensitive to the cultural background of the student. Choose subjects within the realm of your students' experience.

4. **Evaluate all answers to one question before going on to the next.**
   This practice prevents a shifting of standards from one question to the next and helps the rater mark more consistently.

5. **Mark only what the student has written.**
   Don't be influenced by other factors in addition to the quality of the work, such as the quality or legibility of the handwriting.

6. **Have a systematic approach for dealing with marking discrepancies.**
   One such approach might be to take the average of the two raters for a small discrepancy and utilize a third rater if there is a big discrepancy.

7. **Get students involved.**
   Get students involved in developing and marking their writing tests. Have them suggest prompts they'd like to write on and get them involved in peer assessment. Share whatever scoring criteria and rubrics you use with students. Transparency can help students internalize the rubric so that it becomes a natural part of their editing process.

8. **Provide students with diagnostic feedback.**
   Use writing assessment results to identify what students can and cannot do well and provide this information to students. With analytic marking scales, you will have access to a profile to give students feedback. With holistic marking scales, be sure to take notes on students' strengths and areas for improvement.

9. **Practice blind or double blind marking.**
   Mark essays without looking at students' names since the general impression we have of our students is a potential form of bias. Some teachers mark on the basis of how well they know the student and his or her abilities. It is not uncommon for a teacher to give a higher score to a poorly written script of a good or above-average student by rationalizing that "Juan is really a good student even though he didn't show it on this essay. Maybe he was tired or not feeling well." This is known as the halo effect. Have students put their names on the back of their papers or issue each student a candidate number to prevent this practice.

10. **Calibrate and recalibrate.**
    The best way to achieve inter-rater reliability is to practice. Start early in the academic year by employing the marking criteria and scale in non-test situations. Make students aware from the outset of the criteria and expectations for their work. Reliability can be increased by using multiple marking, which reduces the scope for error that is inherent in a single score.

Extension Activity

Mr. Knott has been asked to contribute a writing prompt for the next midterm test. The course objectives focused on description. Here is the prompt he developed. What aspects of the prompt are good? What aspects of the prompt might prove problematic?

E3 MIDTERM EXAM
WRITING SECTION
VERSION C

Student Name: _____   Teacher: _____

I.D. Number: _____   Period/Class Time: _____

WRITING: **DESCRIPTION** | 10 pts. total |

Write a detailed description of the petrol pump in the picture.

Here is Ms. Wright's review of Mr. Knott's writing prompt:

To: Mr. Knott
From: Ms. Wright
RE: Feedback on Your Writing Test Contribution
Date: October 1, 2006

    First of all, let me thank you for your contribution to the midterm exam. In this memo, I'd like to briefly describe what I liked about your test and what I think needs to be improved upon. Let's start with the positive ☺. You have followed our writing specifications that asked for a description of a commonly known object. You also provided glosses for vocabulary that you felt might prove difficult for students. I also like the fact that you included the weighting (10 pts.) of the writing task on the student paper. However, there are a few things that I think might be problematic for our students. The authenticity of describing a gas pump might be inappropriate for students. Most of our students don't drive yet, and I think we should ask them to describe an object that they have some familiarity with and that they might actually describe in real-life contexts. An example might be a computer or laptop. Also, your usage of the British English term *petrol* and metric measurements might be confusing to students. Finally, I feel the rubric should be more detailed. In your next draft of this test, please give students an idea of how much information (i.e., word count, number of details) that you'd like them to include.

    I look forward to seeing your next draft by Wednesday, the 3rd. Thanks for your hard work.

    Regards,
    Ms. Wright

5 Assessing Listening

How important is listening in your school's assessment of your learners?		
(A) **Intensive English Program, Community College, University (-Bound) Program:** Good listening skills are important for academic success, so emphasis is placed on listening skills in the curriculum. Similarly, exams such as the TOEFL® and IELTS™ test listening.	(B) **Conversation Classes, Non-academic Programs, Survival Classes:** Because these programs focus on conversation, the curricula will emphasize speaking and listening, which means that any kind of assessment will also emphasize these two areas. In general, however, more overt emphasis is given to speaking than to listening.	(C) **K–12:** Listening is not "taught" and is therefore not assessed in any formal way in K–12, at least not in the way it is emphasized and assessed in English language programs. However, K–12 teachers are at the forefront for providing English language input for their ELLs. In interacting with their learners in English, K–12 teachers are sometimes the students' main source of native English interaction. Because teachers are constantly making sure that their ELLs have understood the daily class lectures and activities, K–12 teachers are engaging in informal assessment of listening on an ongoing basis.

The assessment of listening abilities is one of the least understood and least developed, yet one of the most important areas of language testing and assessment (Alderson & Bachman, 2001, p. x). In fact, Nunan (2002) calls listening comprehension "the poor cousin amongst the various language skills."

As teachers we recognize the importance of teaching and then assessing the listening skills of our students, but—for a number of reasons—we are often unable to do this effectively. One reason for this is that the listening process is internal and not subject to direct study and observation. To learn to speak, students must first learn to understand the spoken language they hear. In the past, educators hypothesized that listening was a passive skill because it could not be observed. In more recent theoretical models, listening is regarded as an active process. Another reason for the past neglect of the listening skill was that the productive skills of writing and speaking were emphasized. In recent years, however, the position on this has changed, and now a much greater emphasis is placed on listening.

Ms. Wright knows that listening is more than just hearing words. She views listening as an active process whereby students receive, construct meaning from, and respond to spoken messages. Because she sees listening as an integral part of the communication process, she is careful not to neglect this important skill. Some of the things she does in order to ensure valid and reliable listening assessment are:

- She consults her specifications before starting the listening test development process.
- She uses a variety of assessment tasks with different listening purposes.
- She ensures that her tasks are reflective of real-life situations and contexts.
- She collects authentic material to use for listening scripts.
- She asks another teacher to record her listening tasks to expose students to other speech models.
- She checks her listening equipment and does a sound check before the test.
- She standardizes her administration procedures between her two classes.
- She varies her question types and puts more emphasis on meaning than on testing details.
- She pays attention to issues like background knowledge and skill contamination.

Models of Listening

According to Nunan (2002), before we can develop appropriate assessment techniques for listening, we must first understand the nature of listening. Two models of listening have been identified in the literature: bottom-up and top-down approaches.

In *bottom-up processing,* listening is believed to be a linear, data-driven process. In other words, comprehension occurs when the listener successfully decodes the spoken text. Thcsc sounds can range from the smallest meaningful units (phonemes) to complete texts. Comprehension occurs in the bottom-up processing view when students take in a word, decode it, and link it with other words to form sentences. These sentences ultimately form meaningful texts. On the other hand, with *top-down* listening, the listener is directly involved with constructing meaning from input. In this process, the student uses background knowledge of the context and situation to make sense of what is heard. We should teach and assess both types of listening.

Approaches to Listening Assessment

Buck (2001) has identified three major approaches to the assessment of listening abilities: discrete point, integrative, and communicative approaches.

The *discrete-point approach* became popular during the 1950s with the advent of the audiolingual method. This approach broke listening into component elements and assessed them separately. Some of the common question types in this approach included phonemic discrimination, paraphrase recognition, and response evaluation. The underlying rationale for the discrete-point approach stemmed from two beliefs: that it was important to be able to isolate one element of language from a continuous stream of speech and that spoken language was believed to be the same as written language, only presented orally.

The *integrative approach* started in the early 1970s. The underlying rationale for this approach is best explained by Oller (1979): "whereas discrete items attempt to test knowledge of language one bit at a time, integrative tests attempt to assess a learner's capacity to use many bits at the same time" (p. 37). Proponents of the integrative approach to listening assessment believed that the whole of language is greater than the sum of its parts. Common question types in this approach were dictation and cloze.

The communicative approach arose at approximately the same time as the integrative approach as a result of the communicative language teaching movement. In this approach, the listener must be able to comprehend the message and then use it in context. Communicative question formats should be authentic in nature.

General versus Academic Listening

Unlike foreign and second language listening in a conversational setting, a major part of listening in a university context involves lecture comprehension. Many observers (Richards, 1983; Rost, 1990; Flowerdew, 1994) have noted differences between general listening and academic listening. In some cases, these differences have important implications for testing.

Early work by Richards (1983) separated general and academic listening on a taxonomy of micro-skills. Richards' taxonomy identified 33 skills involved in general listening as well as 18 academic listening micro-skills. Richards' general listening micro-skills include clustering; recognizing redundancy; comprehending reduced forms; comprehending hesitations, pauses, false starts, and corrections; understanding colloquial language; processing prosodic features; understanding and using rules of conversational interaction. Richards observed that another set of higher-level micro-skills is necessary in academic listening contexts, including the listener's ability to:

- identify the purpose and scope of a lecture, the lecture topic, and its logical development
- understand the relationship among discourse units (main versus supporting details)
- recognize the lexical terms related to the topic
- recognize markers of cohesion and intonation in a lecture
- detect the speaker's attitude toward the subject
- recognize digressions and non-verbal cues of emphasis

Considerations in Designing Listening Tasks

Before attempting to design a listening test, teachers should consult the course objectives and the listening test specifications that will provide information about objectives, formats, and themes. The tasks should reflect those that occur in real-life situations, and the language used should be natural. As always, the students should be able to use background knowledge to make sense of the test tasks and items. The primary focus of items should generally be on meaning rather than on form.

Background Knowledge

Background or prior knowledge needs to be taken into account because research suggests that background knowledge affects comprehension and test performance. However, take care to ensure that students are not able to answer test questions based on their background knowledge rather than on their comprehension.

Testers can control for background knowledge in one of three ways. First, test designers can ensure students have an equal amount of background knowledge by writing listening tests that exploit specific course materials. Second, they can provide students with the requisite background knowledge during testing via advanced organizers or practice prompts. Third, test writers can use topics that are unfamiliar to the entire student population. In any case, an attempt to standardize the presence or absence of background knowledge should be made in any listening text that purports to be a valid indicator of comprehension.

Test Content

The test specification might provide you with information about the following:

- text types (i.e., narrative, descriptive, etc.)
- speech types to be used (i.e., phrases, single utterances, two-person dialogues, multi-participant dialogue, monologues)
- mode of input (audio, video, live reader)
- varieties of English to be used
- scripted or unscripted input
- length of input (in time or number of exchanges for dialogues)

Texts

Some teachers feel that the unavailability of suitable texts is listening comprehension's most pressing issue because creating scripts that have the characteristics of oral language is not an easy task. In desperation, teachers take a reading text and transform it into a listening script, resulting in contrived and inauthentic listening tasks because written texts often lack the redundant features that are so important in helping us understand speech. A better strategy is to look for texts you like and then infuse oral characteristics into them.

Start by doing an inventory of the topics in a course and collect appropriate material well in advance of exam construction. Some strategies to help you infuse oral characteristics into reading texts are:

- Insert an oral marker at the beginning: "Today I am going to talk about. . . . "
- Spoken language typically uses less complex structures than written text, so change complex sentences into shorter ones.
- Insert devices that help you buy time to plan what to say next (pauses and fillers like *um, err, ah*).
- Use coordinating conjunctions like *and, but,* or *so* instead of ones like *although* and *whereas.*
- Read aloud what you have written to see if it sounds natural.
- If you work from a recording, make a tape script. If you work from a tape script, make a recording.
- Build in pausing, redundancy, and other features of oral texts (false starts, ungrammaticality, hesitations).

Whenever possible try to use samples of authentic speech to assess listening. Other good text sources include radio, television, pre-recorded teaching materials, pod casts, Internet, and teacher-produced materials.

Vocabulary

Research recommends that students must know between 90–95 percent of the words to understand a text/script (Nation, 1990). Indeed the level of the vocabulary that you utilize in your scripts can affect the difficulty and hence the comprehension of students. If your institution employs word lists, it is recommended that you seed vocabulary from your own word lists into listening scripts whenever possible. To determine the vocabulary profile of your text/script, go to *www.er.uqam.ca/nobel/r21270/textools/web_vp.html* for Vocabulary Profiler, user friendly software developed by Paul Nation and maintained by Tom Cobb. By simply pasting your text into the program, you will receive information about the percentage of words that come from Nation's 1,000 Word List, the words that come from the second 1,000 word families, words from the Academic Word List, and words that are not found in these lists. Here is a sample output done on a short text:

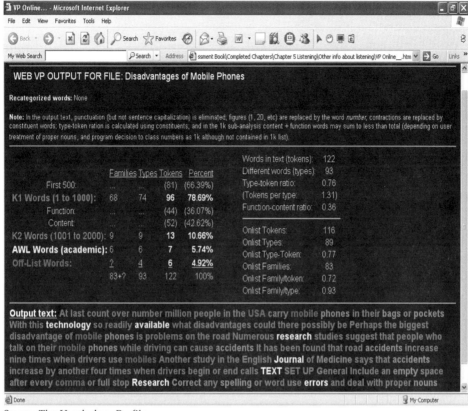

Source: The Vocabulary Profiler.

Another thing to remember about vocabulary is that lexical overlap can affect difficulty. Lexical overlap refers to when words used in the passage are used in the questions and response options (Buck, 2001, p. 153). When words from the passage are used in the correct answer or key, the question is easier. The question becomes more difficult if lexical overlap occurs from the passage/script to the distractors. A final thought on vocabulary is that unknown vocabulary should never occur as the correct answer.

Test Structure

In any test, start with an easy question. This will lower students' test anxiety by relaxing them at the outset of the test. Within a listening test, it is important to test as wide of a range of skills as possible. Questions should be ordered as they are heard in the passage, and items should be spaced out in the passage for good content coverage. It is recommended that no content from the first 15–20 seconds of the recording be tested to allow students to adjust to the listening. Many teachers only include content that is easy to test, such as dates and numbers, so be sure to assess a full range of listening skills. Include some para-phrased content and inferencing tasks to challenge students.

Formats

Students should never be exposed to a new format in a testing situation. If new formats are to be used, practice them in a teaching situation and then introduce them into your testing repertoire. Objective formats like multiple choice questions (MCQs) and true/false (T/F) are often used because they are reliable and easy to mark and analyze. When using these formats, give three response options instead of four for MCQs and drop the NG option from T/F/NG. Memory plays a significant role in listening comprehension. Since students do not have repeated access to the input text, more options add to the memory load and affect the difficulty of the task and question. Visuals are often used as part of listening comprehension assessment. When using them as input, use clear copies that reproduce well.

Item Writing

Once you have decided on the texts and formats you are going to use, it is time to think about the individual test items. Listen to the passage and note areas you want students to understand from the input text. When you have done this, you are ready to start constructing items. Place test items sufficiently far apart in the test so that students have time to respond to one item without missing the next. For example, if answers fall too closely together in the text, students can miss one and find themselves listening for responses that have long since passed.

Frame each new section with an advance organizer to help develop the context and activate student's background knowledge. These examples prepare students for the listening texts:

> Task 1: Listen to the interview with Dr. Peter Davidson, a specialist in sports medicine. He will give you his views on the advantages and disadvantages of Extreme Sports. Then answer the questions.

> Task 2: Mr. and Mrs. Rollins, a young couple from New York City, are discussing their summer plans. Listen to their conversation and then answer the questions.

If you are using a script, build in and record specific instructions so that students know exactly how long they have for each step: The following is a sample of pre-recorded instructions for a listening test.

> You have one minute to read the questions.
> Now start listening.
>> Students hear Task 1 recording.
> You have one minute to read the questions.
> Now start listening.
>> Students hear Task 1 recording.
> You have 30 seconds to write your answers
> Now listen again.
>> Students hear Task 1 again.

Timing

The length of a listening test is generally determined by one of two things: the length of the tape or the number of repetitions of the texts. Most published listening tests do not require attention to timing. The proctor simply inserts the tape or CD into the machine, and the test is over when a pre-recorded *This is the end of the listening test* statement is played. For teacher-produced listening tests, the timing of a test will usually be determined by how many times the test-takers are permitted to hear each passage. Proficiency tests like the TOEFL® and IELTS™ allow students to hear the listening input passages one time, whereas achievement tests usually repeat the input twice. Buck (2001) recommends that if you are assessing main idea, input should be heard once, and if you are assessing detail, input should be heard twice. According to Carroll (1972), listening tests should not exceed 30 minutes.

Remember to give students time to pre-read the questions before the test and answer the questions throughout the test. If students are required to transfer their answers from the test paper to an answer sheet, extra time to do this should be built into the exam.

Skill Contamination

Skill contamination is the idea that a test-taker must use other language skills to answer questions on a listening test. For example, a test taker must first <u>read</u> the question and then <u>write</u> the answer. Whereas skill contamination used to be viewed negatively in the testing literature, it is now viewed more positively and termed *skill integration.*

Techniques for Assessing Listening Comprehension

Phonemic Discrimination

In this task, the student listens to one word spoken in isolation or in a one-sentence context and then tries to identify which word was said. Usually this task is done with minimal pairs, two words that differ in only one phoneme such as *ship/sheep, tank/thank,* or *live/leave.* Here is an example of a phoneme discrimination task used in context:

> Students hear: *He intends to get a new ship next month.*

> Students read and circle the correct response:
> He intends to get a new (ship/sheep) next month.

Paraphrase Recognition

Paraphrase recognition requires students to listen to a statement and then select the option closest in meaning to the statement. Consider this example:

> Students hear: *John nailed his presentation yesterday.*

> Students read and select the best paraphrase:
> A. John used nails at work yesterday.
> B. John's presentation was very successful.
> C. John injured himself after his presentation yesterday.

Objective Formats

Objective formats like MCQs and T/F can be used to assess listening content. Here is an example of both:

Students hear: *The newly married couple took a much-needed break at a hotel last weekend.*

Students read: The couple got married last weekend.

T. F. (F is the answer.)

Students hear: *What would you like to do this weekend?*

Students read: A. Yes, I would.
B. Just relax.**
C. About two days.
D. In five minutes.

** correct answer

Short Answer Questions

Teachers can use short answer question formats to assess listening, provided that the question is short and straightforward.

Students hear: *Last year I spent some time hiking in Vancouver. It was one of the most restful yet energetic vacations I've ever had. Most days we spent about five hours walking and then we set up camp. At the campsite, we read novels and the latest newspapers until the sun went down around 7. After that, we helped prepare the meals.*

Students read and respond: How many hours a day did she

walk? _____

What did she do at night? _____

_____

Cloze

In a listening cloze, students listen to a passage while referring to a written transcript of the text in which several words have been deleted. Students are asked to fill in the blanks while listening.

Students hear: *Every year at this time, the Harris Poll asks people to name their favorite leisure-time activities and how much time they have for their leisure, as well as how much time they spend working—*

including school and keeping house. Reading (28 percent), TV watching (20 percent), spending time with family and kids (12 percent), fishing (12 percent), and gardening (10 percent) are the nation's favorite ways of using their leisure time, all relatively unchanged from the results over the last few years.

Students read and fill in the gaps:

Every year at this time, *The Harris Poll* asks people to name their _____ and how much time they have for their leisure, as well as how much time they spend working— _____. Reading (28 percent), TV watching (_____ percent) spending time with family and _____ (12 percent), fishing (12 percent), and _____ (10 percent) are the nation's favorite ways of using their leisure time, all relatively _____ from the results over the last few years.

Dictation

Dictation has been used to assess language skills for a number of years. In fact, testers classify dictation as an integrative test because it assesses a wide range of skills. To do a dictation with your students, you will need to find a short text of 50–100 words, which you will read three times. You read it once at normal speed. The second reading is done by breaking the text into meaningful units or bursts. The last reading is done at normal speed with no breaks. Students listen during the first reading for the gist of the text and write down what they hear during the second reading. The third reading allows students to check their work and fill in any gaps.

First reading at natural speed with no pauses:

Students go to university to get an education and find a good job. A CV or curriculum vitae is an essential job search tool. A CV is a document that lists your contact details, education, work history, skills, and achievements. A well-written CV is necessary to promote yourself to future employers. According to career advisors, students need to start working on their CVs as soon as they begin college. They recommend that CVs be no longer than two to three pages. Most importantly CVs should be free of spelling and grammar mistakes. Things like this can make a bad impression on future employers.

Second reading with breaks at // and at a slower speed:

Students go to university // to get an education // and find a good job. // A CV or curriculum vitae // is an essential job search tool. // A CV is a document // that lists your contact details, // education, work history, // skills, and achievements. // A well-written CV // is necessary to promote yourself // to future employers. // According to career advisors, // students need to start working // on their CVs as soon as they begin college. // They recommend that CVs // be no longer than two to three pages. // Most importantly // CVs should be free of spelling // and grammar mistakes. // Things like this // can make a bad impression // on future employers.

Third reading at normal speed with no pauses:

Students go to university to get an education and find a good job. A CV or curriculum vitae is an essential job search tool. A CV is a document that lists your contact details, education, work history, skills, and achievements. A well-written CV is necessary to promote yourself to future employers. According to career advisors, students need to start working on their CVs as soon as they begin college. They recommend that CVs be no longer than two to three pages. Most importantly CVs should be free of spelling and grammar mistakes. Things like this can make a bad impression on future employers.

Information Transfer Tasks

Information transfer tasks require students to transfer information they have heard to a chart or visual. Common examples of information transfer tasks used in the assessment of listening are filling in a form or a timetable, labeling a graph, finding something on a map, and following instructions. Here is a sample form-filling activity:

Listen to the conversation between Mrs. Doyle and John Evans who saw a job advertisement in the newspaper. The call for applications ends today. Help Mrs. Doyle, the company secretary, fill in John's application over the phone.

Mrs. Doyle: Good afternoon, Jumbo Electronics. May I help you?

John: Hello, I'm John Evans, and I'd like to inquire about the technician position advertised in the paper. Has the position been filled?

Mrs. Doyle: No, it hasn't, but the call for applications closes at end of business today.

John: What! That's an hour away. I live on the other side of town, and I'll never make it to the office on time in this traffic!

Mrs. Doyle: Not to worry! You can email me all your documents, and we can fill in the application over the phone.

John: Great! What do you need to know?

Mrs. Doyle: Let's start with your full name.

John: That's John Gilbert Evans.

Mrs. Doyle: Can you spell your last name please?

John: Certainly. E-V-A-N-S.

Mrs. Doyle: Your address and telephone number please.

John: 847 Main Street, Cumberland, Maryland.

Mrs. Doyle: What is the zip code on that?

John: Oh, sorry. 28601.

Mrs. Doyle: Just a few more questions. Do you have a phone number in case we need to contact you for an interview?

John: Let me give you my cell phone number. It's 301-777-0987.

Mrs. Doyle: And what day would be best for an interview?

John: Well, I'm willing to come in any time you need me to but probably Tuesday morning would be best for me.

Mrs. Doyle: Thanks, Mr. Evans. I'll get this up to personnel right away. You'll be hearing from us soon.

John: Thanks for all your help. Bye!

Help Mrs. Doyle fill in John's application:

Jumbo Electronics

Job Application Form

Name of applicant: _____
　　　　　　　　　　　Last　　　　　　　　*First*　　　　*Middle Initial*

Address: _____

City/State: _____ Zip Code: _____

Telephone: _____ _____ home

　　　　　　　　　　　　　　　　　　 _____ work

　　　　　　　　　　　　　　　　　　 _____ cell

Preferred Interview Day/Time:　 _____ Saturday

　　　　　　　　　　　　　　 _____ Monday　　 _____ AM

　　　　　　　　　　　　　　 _____ Tuesday　　 _____ PM

　　　　　　　　　　　　　　 _____ Wednesday

　　　　　　　　　　　　　　 _____ Thursday

　　　　　　　　　　　　　　 _____ Friday

Note-Taking

Note-taking is an authentic task in academic programs. Students are actively involved as they write key information they understand from the input text. Note-taking can be handled in two ways. Students listen and simultaneously fill out the question paper or take notes. With this task, note-taking can be as guided or as unstructured as you want. Alternatively, students listen to the text and take notes, which they then use to answer questions.

Sample Tape Script for Note-Taking Task

Good morning, students. In today's lecture I'm going to tell you about a place that I find really fascinating. How many of you have heard about or seen pictures of a place called Angel Falls? Angel Falls is famous because it is the world's highest waterfall. It is 979 meters high. It is located on the Churun River in Canaima National Park in Venezuela. This magnificent waterfall was not known to the world until its discovery in 1933 by an American pilot called Jimmy Angel. Jimmy was flying a plane that was searching for gold when he discovered the falls for the first time. But he couldn't land his plane at that time. In 1937, he returned and landed his plane at the top of the waterfall. The plane got damaged during the landing, and he had to walk through the rainforest to the nearest village for help. As you have probably already guessed, the falls are currently named "Angel Falls" after him.

Not surprisingly, because of their height and beauty, the falls are one of Venezuela's top tourist attractions. Despite their popularity, they are difficult to get to. A trip to the falls requires a short plane trip to Canaima. Then you must take a boat trip to reach the falls. For an easier way to see them, it is also possible to take a tour that flies past the falls. If you're planning on taking a trip there, though, you must pay attention to the weather because the falls cannot be seen on cloudy days. During the dry season from December to March there is less water falling over them, but you have a better chance that it won't be cloudy.

Students fill out the chart based on information from the lecture.

What is the topic of the lecture?	Angel Falls
Why are the falls famous?	
In which country are they located?	
When were they discovered?	
How do you visit the falls? (name one way)	
What is a bad time to visit Angel Falls?	

Listening Test Delivery

The physical characteristics of the test setting or venue can affect the validity and/or reliability of the test. Exam rooms must have good acoustics and minimal background noise. The equipment used in test administrations should be well maintained and checked out beforehand. In addition, an AV technician should be available to correct any problems with the equipment during the administration.

The way a listening test is administered and delivered can impact the results as well. Examples of commonly used modes of delivery in listening assessment include audiotapes, videotapes, CD-ROMs, and live readers. Differences in the mode used influence the students' degree of comprehension. Research shows that students comprehend less when paralinguistic cues are unavailable (Kellerman, 1992), as would be the case in audiotaped scripts. To produce more extemporaneous listening recordings, use available programs on your computer like Sound Recorder or shareware like *Audacity*® and PureVoice® to record scripts for use as listening assessments in the classroom.

Certain speaker characteristics can also effect listening assessment. Problems can arise when speakers with different accents, styles, speech rates, or degrees of professional or social status deliver the listening text. A number of speaker variables have been identified that significantly affect listening comprehension in L2 students, including rate of speech (Tauroza & Allison, 1990), perceived expertness of the speaker, gender (Markham, 1988), dialect of the speaker (Tauroza, 1997), and pauses (Blau, 1991).

Non-standard procedures can result in unreliable test scores. Common procedural factors that can influence results include the number of text repetitions given, length of time allowed to complete the task, undue speaker stress or intonation used to cue correct answers, policies regarding unscripted mistakes, and false starts in live reader situations. Teachers should attempt to standardize the delivery of all listening assessment. Inconsistencies in the delivery of a listening test can unfairly help or hinder student performance.

Recording Voiceovers

Anyone recording a segment for a listening test should receive training and practice beforehand. In large-scale testing, it is advisable to use a mixture of genders, accents, and dialects. To be fair for all students, listening voiceovers should match the demographics of the student and teacher population. Other important issues to consider are the use of non-native speakers of English for voiceovers and the speed of delivery. Whoever records listening test voiceovers, whether native or non-native speaker, should speak clearly and enunciate carefully. The speed of delivery of a listening test should be consistent with the level of the students and the materials used for instruction. If your institution espouses a communicative approach, then the speed of delivery for listening assessments should be native or near native delivery. The delivery of the test should be standard for all test-takers. If live readers are used, they should practice reading the script before the test and standardize with other readers.

Scoring

Scoring listening tests poses numerous challenges to the teacher. Dichotomous scoring (questions that are either right or wrong) is easier and more reliable. However, it does not lend itself to many communicative formats such as notetaking. Other issues include whether to deduct points for grammar, spelling mistakes, or non-adherence to word counts. When more than one teacher is marking a listening test, calibration or standardization training should be completed to ensure fairness to all students.

Ten Things to Remember about Assessing Listening

Valid and reliable testing of listening comprehension is a complex process. Keep these points in mind.

1. **Assess listening comprehension even though it is difficult to assess.**
   One reason for the neglect of listening assessment materials is the unavailability of culturally appropriate listening materials suitable for ESL/EFL contexts. The biggest challenges for teaching and assessing listening comprehension concern the production of listening materials. Indeed, listening comprehension assessment is often avoided because of the time, effort, and expense required to develop, rehearse, record, and produce high-quality audiotapes or CDs.

2. **Reading texts must be converted to listening texts.**
   A written text lacks oral features. The closer a text is to oral language, the more appropriate it will be to assess students' listening comprehension.

3. **Give credit for what students know.**
   Don't deduct for spelling or grammar mistakes when your focus is on listening comprehension.

4. **Don't forget the importance of background knowledge.**
   Because students do not have multiple passes at the text, there needs to be sufficient contextualization prior to listening. To facilitate schema activation, set the context of the listening in the instructions.

5. **Don't just test what is easy to test.**
   Many teachers focus their test items on local information (e.g., numbers, dates, places) because these detail-focused items are easier to write than items that focus on meaning. Make sure your major focus is on meaning. Include higher-order thinking skills as well.

6. **Give students a reason for listening.**
   The purpose of the listening activity should resemble those in real-life situations. Input should have a communicative purpose. In other words, the listener must have a reason for listening.

7. **Don't expect full comprehension.**
   Teachers should not expect students to remember everything they hear; students often comprehend without being able to remember content.

8. **Accept that skill contamination will occur.**
   In a perfect world, reading or writing would never interfere with the assessment of the listening skill. In reality, the successful completion of practically every listening test requires competence in other language skill areas. However, if the aim is to test listening, students should not be asked to read or write too much.

9. **Assess all types of listening (top down/bottom up and general/academic).**
   Vary your measures where listening comprehension is concerned.

10. **Don't forget the cornerstones of good testing practice.**
    In listening, as in all the other skills, teachers should be guided by the cornerstones of testing: validity, reliability, practicality, washback, authenticity, transparency, and security.

Extension Activity

To prepare his students for their upcoming listening test, Mr. Knott has created a practice guided note-taking task. Take a look at his transcript and assessment task, and note its strengths and weaknesses.

Mr. Knott's Tape Script for Note-Taking Task

Listening Script: New Tuskland

Today I am going to talk about a country called New Tuskland. I will discuss the geographical features, animal life, climate, and resources of the country. New Tuskland is located in the northern part of the Gumayan continent. It shares borders with Inlanda, Gammaland, and the Azure Ocean. It is a large country with an area of about 213,230 square kilometers.

New Tuskland has a wide variety of geographical features. There is a long coastline that is located on the Azure Ocean. In the eastern part of the country there are high mountains. A large lake and river are found in the south. In addition to these geographical features, New Tuskland has many modern tourist resorts along the north coast with several 5-star hotels.

Many tourists come to New Tuskland to watch whales. They take boats from the harbor near the capital city called Seeb. The whales swim near the island.

The climate of New Tuskland differs from region to region depending on the altitude. Along the coast and in the mountains, the climate is hot and rainy. The average daily temperature is between 15 and 50 degrees Celsius. The rainy season occurs from May to November.

New Tuskland is very rich in natural resources. The most important natural resource of New Tuskland is polystyrene. Polystyrene is a substance made from hydrocarbons and is used in the production of aeronautical supplies. It is the main export of the country. Natural gas, gold, and forest land are also important resources for New Tuskland.

In summary, New Tuskland is a land with many varied geographical features and resources. It welcomed nearly half a million tourists last year.

English Listening Test

Name: _____   Teacher: _____

I.D. Number: _____   Date: _____

New Tuskland

Listen to the talk about New Tuskland and then fill in the correct information. Use the map on the back of the test paper to help you (5 points).

Country	
Location	
Size	1. 2.
Geographical Features	
Weather	
Wild animals	• •
Most important resource	

Ms. Wright's Review of Mr. Knott's Test

Strengths:

- It is an authentic guided listening task.
- It is academic in nature.
- The content is indicative of a geography lecture.
- Points are included in the rubric.
- Answer content is fairly spread out in the text.
- Questions are mostly in the order of how they are heard.
- The instructions for the task are fairly explicit.

Weaknesses:

(Tape Script)

- Authenticity is the biggest problem here. Obviously New Tuskland is an imaginary place. There are enough places in the world that students don't know about, so it is not necessary to make up places.
- It reads like a written text (only exception is "Today I am going to talk about. . . . ").
- The number of points allocated to the task is not enough for the number of questions posed; the result will be in 1/4 points.

(Questions)

- Extraneous clue on the first item; New Tuskland is located on the test paper not once but twice.
- The location question does not specify how much information should be written down; both of the following propositions are keyable:

  —"located in the northern part of the Gumayan continent"

  —"It shares borders with Inlanda, Gammaland, and the Azure Ocean."

  Because no specific info is given on how much information is required, some students will write only one of the above-mentioned keys; others will write both. When it comes time to score, teachers will feel inclined to give those students who wrote more higher marks, thereby disadvantaging students who in fact adequately answered the question.

- For the Geographical Features question, no indication is made as to how many are wanted. The only indication that more than one answer is wanted is the plural "s" on Features.
- For the Weather question, the term *climate* is used in the text.
- The Wild Animals question implies that two responses are wanted but only one (whale) is in the text.
- The key to the Most Valuable Resource is *polystyrene*, a low-frequency word that is difficult even for the native speaker to spell. Unless this word is part of the unit vocabulary list, the teacher will have to accept virtually any answer that begins with *poly-*.

6 Assessing Speaking

How important is speaking in your school's assessment of your learners?		
(A) **Intensive English Program, Community College, University (-Bound) Program:** Prior to the new TOEFL®, speaking was not accorded much importance in these programs because the TOEFL® did not assess speaking. However, the new iBT® TOEFL® assesses several speaking samples from ESL learners. Programs are now implementing speaking assessments of various types, often to mimic the TOEFL®. This shift means short tests of impromptu speaking (normally 60–90 seconds), speaking in reaction to a listening passage, and speaking in reaction to a reading passage.	(B) **Conversation Classes, Non-academic Programs, Survival Classes:** Because these programs focus on conversation, the curricula will emphasize speaking and listening, which means that any kind of assessment will also emphasize these two areas. In general, however, more overt emphasis is given to speaking than to listening. Some programs have an exit interview that requires the student to speak in response to several questions or prompts.	(C) **K–12:** Speaking is not "taught" and is therefore not assessed in any formal way in K–12. However, K–12 teachers are at the forefront for providing English language input for their ELLs. K–12 teachers are constantly monitoring their ELLs' speaking ability in English by engaging in informal assessment.

As in daily life, speaking is an important channel of communication in a general English program. When testing this skill, we want to simulate real-life situations in which students engage in conversation, ask and answer questions, and give information. In an academic English program, the emphasis may shift to participating in class discussions and debates or giving academic presentations. In a business English course, students might develop telephone skills, make reports, and interact in common situations involving meetings, travel, and sales. Whatever the teaching focus, valid assessment should reflect the course objectives.

Ms. Wright knows the importance most students place on being able to speak proficiently, so she assesses her students' speaking abilities both in class and in a formal speaking exam. Some of the things she does in order to ensure valid and reliable speaking assessment are:

- She starts any speaking assessment with an unassessed warm-up to reduce nervousness.
- She conducts her speaking exams with another teacher so that each has a specific role.
- She uses a range of assessment tasks.
- She focuses on both fluency and accuracy when marking students' speech.
- She records exams so that she has a record of them for later reference.
- She limits the number of speaking exams per day to ensure intra-rater reliability.
- She conducts regular calibration sessions with other teachers to ensure inter-rater reliability.

Heaton (1995, p. 88) points out that speaking is "an extremely difficult skill to test, as it is far too complex a skill to permit any reliable analysis to be made for the purpose of objective testing." The greatest challenges are resource requirements and reliability, including the perceived subjectivity in grading. Lack of time, number of students, lack of available tests, and administrative difficulties are other pressing concerns. In addition, practicality issues for reliability of the marking often arise as raters must be trained, and this training can be very time consuming. For all these reasons, many teachers do not even attempt to assess speaking. However, the assessment of spoken language has evolved dramatically over the last several decades from tests of oral grammar and pronunciation to tests of genuine communication, and now to integrative speaking tasks on high-stakes tests like the TOEFL® and TOEIC®.

Why Test Speaking?

Despite the difficulties associated with assessing the speaking skill, there are important reasons that speaking should receive as much attention in assessment as the other language skills. In communicative language teaching, speaking is a prominent component of the language curriculum (Folse, 2006; Jones, 2005). If we value communication skills, we must assess them or we send a double message to our students about what we consider to be important. Furthermore, with English now a global language, a large percentage of the world's language learners study English in order to develop proficiency in speaking. In the interests of promoting clear international communications, we need to recognize the importance of spoken English by testing students' progress.

Theory of Speaking Assessment

Harris (1977, p. 81) notes that speaking is a complex skill requiring the simultaneous use of different abilities that often develop at different rates—namely pronunciation, grammar, vocabulary, fluency, and comprehension. These abilities still underlie the assessment of speaking, but now more attention is paid to contextual and interactional factors.

Canale and Swain (1980) argue that there are four competencies underlying speaking ability:

- *Grammatical competence:* includes knowledge of grammar, vocabulary, and mechanics (basic sounds of letters and syllables, pronunciation of words, intonation and stress) (Scarcella & Oxford, 1992, p. 141)
- *Discourse competence:* concerned with relationships beyond the sentence level, rules of cohesion and coherence, holding communication together in a meaningful way
- *Sociolinguistic competence:* applying knowledge of what is expected socially and culturally by users of the target language
- *Strategic competence:* "the way learners manipulate language in order to meet communicative goals" (Brown, H.D., 1994, p. 228); the ability to know when to take the floor, how to keep a conversation going or end it, and how to resolve communication breakdowns

Categories of Oral Skills

Weir (1993) categorizes oral skills as speaking skills that are part of a repertoire of routines for exchanging information or interacting, and improvisational skills such as negotiating meaning and managing the interaction. The routine skills are largely associated with language functions and the spoken language required in certain situations like ordering food in a restaurant or asking for directions to a museum. By contrast, the improvisational skills are more general and may be brought into play at any time for clarification, to keep a conversation flowing, to change topics, or to take turns. It is the teacher's task to decide which speaking skills are most germane to a particular program and then create a variety of assessment tasks. It is also common to weight some skills more heavily than others.

Differences between Writing and Speaking

Before we focus specifically on assessing speaking, it is necessary to understand some of the differences between the two productive language skills—writing and speaking. We have already seen that subjectivity is a major issue in grading writing and that is also the case for assessing speaking. As with writing, there is the issue of whether to grade speaking holistically or analytically. However, as

Writing	Speaking
Full, complex, and well-organized sentences	Incomplete, simply and loosely organized sentences
Information densely packed	Simpler discourse with less information
Use of specific vocabulary	Use of more general vocabulary
Use of discourse markers to help the reader	Frequent use of fillers to facilitate speech
Text written for an unseen audience	Face-to-face communication
A relatively solitary process	Negotiation of meaning between two or more people
Alterations and crossings out kept to a minimum	Alterations, corrections, and miscues are very common
Reference can easily be made to what has been written previously	Memory limitations are important as speech is transitory

Source: Jones, W. (2005). Assessing students' oral proficiency. In D. Lloyd, P. Davidson, & C. Coombe (Eds.), *The fundamentals of language assessment: A practical guide for teachers in the Gulf* (pp. 75–86). Dubai: TESOL Arabia Publications, p. 77.

you can see in the chart on page 114, writing and speaking differ significantly. According to Jones (2005, p. 77), these differences "are fundamental to our understanding of the construct of speaking and any assessment of this skill must take these features into consideration."

In contrast to writing, speaking is more ephemeral unless measures are taken to record student performance. Yet the presence of recording equipment can negatively influence students' performance and often recording is not practical or feasible.

Special Issues in Speaking Assessment

Logistically, the administration of speaking exams to large numbers of students can be overwhelming in terms of time and resources. With large classes, it is unrealistic to test speaking individually. For example, to test a class of 30 students individually, it would take more than four class periods to administer a 10- to 15-minute speaking exam. One solution is to develop assessments that test more than one student at a time, yet allow each student some opportunities to speak individually. Another solution is to test, formally only a few times during a course but to use continuous assessment of students during normal classroom activities.

Another phenomenon in speaking assessment is that sometimes a student can score higher on exams because of having an outgoing personality. Take care to evaluate a student on what was said in the exam, not on personality.

Designing Speaking Assessments
Prior Considerations

A number of factors need to be considered *before* designing speaking assessments. One is whether to focus more on fluency or accuracy. On the one hand, fluency is important for students, but if there are many errors, that might impede comprehension. We recommend that you focus equally on fluency and accuracy. Ask yourself whether the mistakes students make impede comprehension or cause a breakdown in communication. If they do not, ignore or play down the problems. One way to ensure that you place an equal focus on both fluency and accuracy is to build this into your assessment criteria. In other words, 50 percent of a student's grade would come from aspects of fluency such as initiating and maintaining communication and 50 percent would be based on how accurately the student spoke.

Teachers also have to decide on which criteria to evaluate. If you espouse an equal emphasis on fluency and accuracy, we recommend the following marking categories: *accuracy* (grammar), *vocabulary, linguistic ability* (pronunciation, intonation, and stress), *fluency* (ability to express ideas), and *content* or ideas. Work with your colleagues to determine the relative weighting of each category to ensure inter-rater reliability. We've all experienced instances where one rater emphasized accuracy in grammar and pronunciation only to be at odds with a colleague who focused on the ability of the speaker to fluently express meaning.

Another factor to consider before you design your assessment is the procedure for grading. Since subjectivity is a major problem in marking speaking exams, a common solution is to use multiple raters. The more teachers you use, the more reliable a test score will be. It is common practice to use two raters with different roles for speaking exams. One teacher, the *interlocutor*, interacts with the student or students being tested. The other teacher, the *assessor*, focuses on writing scores and making notes. At the end of the test after the candidates leave, the two raters either discuss their suggested marks and negotiate an agreed-upon score or take an average of the two marks. For reliability, interlocutors should work from a script so that all students get similar questions framed in the same way. In general, the teacher or assessor should keep in the background and only intercede if truly necessary.

The grading process is greatly simplified if the assessor uses a scoring sheet with the criteria for assessment and their relative weights. A clear, easy-to-use grading sheet reduces note-taking and keeps the grading criteria ever present. If the speaking assessment is a formative exam, have a section on the sheet with comments that can be used later for feedback to the student. Here is a checklist for two teachers assessing two students at one time. Note grading criteria and section for feedback.

Upper Intermediate English
Speaking Assessment Checklist
Date: _____   Time: _____
Interlocutor: _____
Assessor: _____

S's Name: _____ ID #: _____

Pass? ☐ yes ☐ no

below average above
☐ ☐ ☐ grammar generally accurate, adequate
           (basic sentences, tenses, vocabulary OK)

☐ ☐ ☐ pronunciation, intonation OK
           (mainly intelligible, appropriate)

☐ ☐ ☐ discourse management
           (maintains flow of conversation)

☐ ☐ ☐ (S can initiate, respond; can maintain, repair)

Problems for remediation:
☐ response inappropriate
☐ S can't initiate, sustain at normal speed
☐ S needs excessive prompting
☐ other: _____

S's Name: _____ ID #: _____

Pass? ☐ yes ☐ no

below average above
☐ ☐ ☐ grammar generally accurate, adequate
           (basic sentences, tenses, vocabulary OK)

☐ ☐ ☐ pronunciation, intonation OK
           (mainly intelligible, appropriate

☐ ☐ ☐ discourse management
           (maintains flow of conversation)

☐ ☐ ☐ interactive communication
           (S can initiate, respond; can maintain, repair)

Problems for remediation:
☐ response inappropriate
☐ S can't initiate, sustain at normal speed
☐ S needs excessive prompting
☐ other: _____

A final concern before designing the assessment is deciding what type of speaking samples to collect from students. Brown and Yule (1983) recommend collecting speaking data with the following characteristics:

- speech that has a purpose
- extended chunks of speech
- speech that is structured or organized
- tasks where the amount of speech is controlled
- tasks where there is a specific number of points of required information

Designing Speaking Assessments

As noted, we recommend that teachers assess speaking in class as well as through individual speaking tests. To get a valid picture of speaking proficiency, use a variety of methods and techniques. We will explore techniques ranging from a traditional formal test to informal techniques you can integrate with other classroom activities. Whatever technique you use, start the speaking assessment with a simple task that puts students at ease so they perform better.

Formal Speaking Assessment Techniques

The speaking test or oral interview is perhaps the most common format for assessing speaking on well-known language examinations. Many institutions schedule formal speaking exams at least once during a course to ensure that all students are tested under reliable and standard conditions. Oral exams/interviews need not be overly long. According to Hughes (2003), each student needs 15 minutes to ensure that the information a rater receives is reliable. For placement purposes, an interview of between five to ten minutes should suffice.

In 1984, Canale proposed a framework for speaking tests that is still in use today. He believed that students perform best when they are led through the following stages:

- **Warm up:** The purpose of this phase is to relax students and lower their anxiety. Students are asked for personal details such as general information about themselves, their likes and dislikes, etc. Assessors can even ask students to spell out something or give numerical sequences (e.g., zip code, telephone number, etc.). The warm-up phase has a dual purpose of putting the students at ease and getting basic information about them. It usually takes a minute or two and is not assessed.

- **Level check:** At this stage, the assessor tries to determine the student's level of speaking proficiency through a series of questions or situational activities. This part of the exam is assessed.

- **Probe:** In this part of the speaking test, the examiner attempts to push the student to the height of his or her speaking ability. Another function can be as a confirmation of the level check. This part of the exam is assessed if the student can go beyond his or her abilities, but it is unscored if a communication breakdown occurs.

- **Wind down:** At this stage of the exam, the examiner once again attempts to relax the student with some easy questions, perhaps about future plans. Typical content during this stage is information about when and where to obtain exam results. This part of the oral exam/interview is not scored.

Variations on the Framework

Students can be tested individually, in pairs, or in groups of three. If more than one student is assessed, it is important to provide time for each individual to speak as well as opportunities for interaction. This set-up makes it possible to test common routine functions as well as a range of improvisational skills. In paired-student oral exams, the examiner has the advantage of hearing students interacting with their peers. However, examiners should take care not to let one student monopolize the conversation.

Regardless of the particular tasks employed, the general flow of the exam will follow the four steps identified by Canale. Here are some common tasks that can be used for the level-check stage.

- **Picture Cue:** Visuals can be very useful in assessing speaking skills. They are especially good for descriptions. In this technique, students are given a picture or photo and must describe what they see. Pictures can be as simple or as elaborate as you want or can illustrate a story. Make sure you give students enough time to look at the picture before you require them to start speaking. Good sources for visuals are newspaper and magazine photographs or advertisements, printed digital photographs, or pictures downloaded from the Internet. The National Geographic website *(http://lava.nationalgeographic.com/cgi-bin/pod/archive.cgi)* is a particularly good source for high-quality photographs for teaching and testing.

  Alternatively, students may have to answer questions about the picture or photograph. This variation is a useful way of focusing on certain structures, functions, or vocabulary. Consider the following example.

Sample Activity

Look at the picture and answer the questions.

Mario's Italian Restaurant

1 spaghetti	9.50
1 steak dinner	14.80
2 salads	6.00
1 soft drink	1.50
1 tomato juice	2.20
	34.00
Thanks! 8% tax	5.44
total	39.44

Source: Folse, K. S. (1996). *Discussion starters: Speaking fluency activities for advanced ESL/EFL students.* Ann Arbor: University of Michigan Press, p. 100.

Questions:

- What kind of food does the restaurant serve?
- Which dish is the most expensive?
- Did the customer leave a tip? If so, how much?
- In your opinion, was the meal expensive? Why? Why not?

An elaboration of the visual technique is to give the student a series of pictures or a cartoon strip and ask her/him to narrate the major events in a story. This approach can be used to elicit sequence markers and a variety of verb tenses.

Sample Activity

Look at the two illustrations and explain what is happening in each.

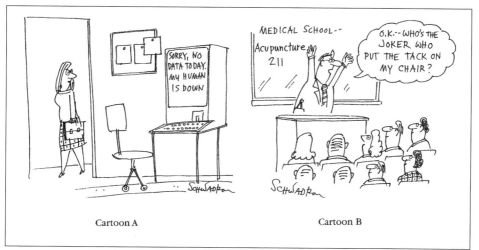

Cartoon A   Cartoon B

Source: Folse, 1996, p. 78.

- **Prepared Monologue:** The teacher provides students with a written topic card. Students have one minute to make notes and then present their remarks on the topic. Possible topics include agreement or disagreement with a controversial statement, extemporaneous topics, or explaining proverbs or idioms.

- **Role play:** Students are given cue cards with information about their "character" and the setting. If there is only one student, the interlocutor role-plays with him or her. If there are two or more students, be certain that the roles they are asked to play are familiar to all and would elicit comparable amounts of speech.

    Some students find it difficult to project themselves into an imaginary situation, and this lack of acting ability may affect reliability. Role plays should not be used on a test unless they have been a normal part of class activities; a good test always reflects actual class content and teaching.

Sample Activity

You buy something from the store and when you get home, you discover it is broken. You take it back to the store and talk with the manager.

- **Information Gap Activity:** One student has information the other lacks and vice versa. Students have to exchange information to see how it fits together. Students work together on a task on which they may have different opinions. They have to reach a conclusion in a limited period of time.

Sample Activity

Students must select a graduation gift for a mutual friend. They are given five pictures of possible gifts to buy. They must discuss which gift to buy and come to an agreement.

Classroom Speaking Assessment Techniques

Oral Presentations

The Icebreaker speech is an ideal first start to the art of oral presentations. It is designed to get students talking about a familiar topic: themselves. It is a 4 to 6 minute speech where the student introduces himself or herself to the rest of the class. The advantage of this speech as a first effort is that it serves as a warm-up and gets the student in front of an audience.

Giving oral presentations is a real-life skill for students in academic and business programs, so presentations are often used for classroom speaking assessment. Oral presentations are not just concerned with language accuracy and fluency. They also include aspects of delivery such as body language, facial expression, eye contact, and gestures. The visual aids and handouts that the student creates and uses are integral parts of the presentation. PowerPoint or other presentation software is often used to highlight the spoken delivery. Here is an example of an analytical grading sheet based on ten components that are considered important in one English program. For each component, a score of ten would be the highest grade and zero the lowest.

Grading Chart for Individual Class Presentation

Student's name: _____ Date: _____

Topic: _____

		Well done							Done poorly			
1.	Content (Relevant, Shows Research)	10	9	8	7	6	5	4	3	2	1	0
2.	Task Fulfilment	10	9	8	7	6	5	4	3	2	1	0
3.	Delivery	10	9	8	7	6	5	4	3	2	1	0
4.	Pronunciation	10	9	8	7	6	5	4	3	2	1	0
5.	Communicative Performance	10	9	8	7	6	5	4	3	2	1	0
6.	Use of Visual Aids	10	9	8	7	6	5	4	3	2	1	0
7.	Organization	10	9	8	7	6	5	4	3	2	1	0
8.	Fielding Questions	10	9	8	7	6	5	4	3	2	1	0
9.	Language (Grammar and Vocabulary)	10	9	8	7	6	5	4	3	2	1	0
10.	Time Management	10	9	8	7	6	5	4	3	2	1	0

Total score = _____ /100

Comments for feedback:

Teacher's Signature: _____

Debate on a Controversial Topic

A debate is a formal public speaking activity where two students or groups of students argue for or against a topic. The topic they debate is called the motion. The student(s) who argues for the motion usually starts the debate with a three-minute speech. The student(s) on the opposing team then has a chance to argue against or rebut the arguments made by the first student(s). Group or team debates in which two teams of four students argue for and against a certain motion are preferred. Three students on each team deliver oral arguments. The remaining student serves as a silent observer who helps formulate the arguments or rebuttal statements.

Sample Debate Topics:

- Cigarette smoking should be banned in all public places.
- The legal driving age should be raised to 21.
- Men and women can never be just friends.

Here is a sample grading form for three students, each of whom is graded individually before a group grade is given.

Grading Chart for Three-Student Debate

The motion: _____

Content	Mark	Speaker 1 Names: _____	Speaker 2 Names: _____	Speaker 3 Names: _____
The speaker developed strong, well-supported arguments and successfully rebutted opponent's argument(s), if applicable.	10/9			
The speaker developed well-supported arguments and quite successfully rebutted opponent's argument(s), if applicable.	8/7			
The speaker developed satisfactory arguments, competently supported, and rebutted a number of the opponent's argument(s), if applicable.	6/5			
The speaker developed weak, poorly supported arguments and tried generally unsuccessfully to rebut opponent's argument(s), if applicable.	4/3			
The speaker developed largely irrelevant arguments and rebutted none of the opponent's argument(s), if applicable.	2/1			

Organization	Mark	Speaker 1	Speaker 2	Speaker 3
The speech was very well organized, clearly signposted, and a pleasure to listen to.	5			
The speech was well organized, well signposted, and easy to listen to.	4			
The speech was organized, signposted, and rather easy to listen to.	3			
The speech was poorly organized, signposted in parts, and slightly difficult to listen to.	2			
The speech was very poorly organized, not signposted, and difficult to listen to.	1			
Presentation and Language Skills	**Mark**	**Speaker 1**	**Speaker 2**	**Speaker 3**
Information was confidently presented using correct grammar and a wide range of appropriate vocabulary in a way that clearly resonated with the audience.	5			
Information was well presented, using almost error-free grammar and a very good range of appropriate vocabulary in a way that resonated with the audience.	4			
Information was satisfactorily presented using mainly correct grammar and an adequate range of appropriate vocabulary in a way that mainly resonated with the audience.	3			
Information was fairly satisfactorily presented using correct grammar and a narrow range of appropriate vocabulary in a way that did not resonate much with the audience.	2			
Information was presented using somewhat correct grammar and a less-than-adequate range of appropriate vocabulary in a way that clearly did not resonate with the audience.	1			

Speaker 1___/20 × 5 = ___%   **Speaker 2** ___/20 × 5 = ___%   **Speaker 3** ___/20 × 5 = ___%

GROUP RESULT = Percentages for Speakers 1 + 2 + 3 divided by 3 = _____%

Reading Aloud

Reading aloud is good for pronunciation practice and assessment, and it can be done with unrelated sentences or connected prose. Give students a chance to look at the passage first. A useful tool for assessing pronunciation is the Accent Inventory, developed by Prator and Robinett (1972). This 155-word paragraph is a diagnostic tool that students can record pre- and post- course. It comes with a checklist of problems on stress and rhythm, intonation, vowel and consonant sounds.

Retelling Stories

Students are asked to report on the contents of a graded reader or a magazine/ newspaper article they have read.

Verbal Essays

Verbal essays require the students to speak for approximately three to five minutes on a specified prepared topic.

Extemporaneous Speaking

Students are given a topic and are asked to speak on it extemporaneously for one to two minutes. Students have no time in which to prepare.

Sample Topics:

- A person you really admire
- A world problem you'd like to solve
- A place you'd really like to visit

Now more than ever, speaking plays an important role on the TOEFL® iBT. The test takes an integrated skills approach that requires students to employ more than one skill at a time. For speaking, the student listens to six questions on audio. Two of the questions are on familiar topics, and the remaining four require the student to listen to or read something and then respond orally. According to the producers of the test, the integrated approach is a more authentic form of speaking assessment.

General Rubric for Assessing Speaking

Thus far, we have presented rubrics for oral presentations (page 123) and debates (pages 124–125). Many teachers, however, prefer to use a more general rubric for these and other speaking tasks, such as role plays, retelling stories, and extemporaneous speaking. For these tasks, we recommend the speaking assessment rubric on page 127.

Speaking Assessment		Name: _____ Date: _____
Category	**Your Score**	**Guide**
Grammar 25 points		24–25 *Excellent.* Few errors; communication of ideas is clear.
		22–23 *Very good.* One or two errors, but communication is mostly clear.
		20–21 *Good.* Several errors in syntax, but main ideas are mostly clear.
		18–19 *Fair.* Noticeable errors that occasionally confuse meaning.
		12–17 *Weak.* Language is marked by errors. Listeners' attention is diverted to the errors rather than the message. Meaning is often unclear or broken.
		0–11 *Unacceptable.* Communication is impeded. Too many errors in this task for a student at this level.
Vocabulary 20 points		20 *Excellent.* Correct selection of words and idioms. Variety of vocabulary.
		18–19 *Very good.* Correct selection of words and idioms. Some variety of vocabulary.
		16–17 *Good.* Mostly correct choice of vocabulary. Meaning is clear.
		14–15 *Fair.* Noticeable vocabulary errors that occasionally confuse meaning. Reliance on simple vocabulary to communicate.
		12–13 *Weak.* Many vocabulary errors. Listeners' attention is diverted to the errors rather than the message. Meaning is often unclear or broken.
		0–11 *Unacceptable.* Too many errors in this task for a student at this level. Communication is impeded.
Fluency 30 points		29–30 *Excellent.* No hesitations at all.
		27–28 *Very good.* Hesitations in one or two places but immediately continued.
		24–26 *Good.* Occasional hesitations but recovered well.
		21–23 *Fair.* Noticeable gaps that catch listeners' attention usually followed by recovery.
		12–20 *Weak.* Several short periods of silence. Several gaps that disrupt the flow of information. Listeners' attention is diverted to the gaps rather than the message.
		0–11 *Unacceptable.* Periods of silence. Gaps without good recovery.
Pronunciation 25 points		24–25 *Excellent.* Few errors; native-like pronunciation.
		22–23 *Very good.* One or two errors, but communication is mostly clear.
		20–21 *Good.* Several pronunciation errors, but main ideas are understood without problem.
		18–19 *Fair.* Noticeable pronunciation errors that occasionally confuse meaning.
		12–17 *Weak.* Language is marked by pronunciation errors. Listeners' attention is diverted to the errors rather than the message. Meaning is often unclear.
		0–11 *Unacceptable.* Too many errors in this task for a student at this level. Communication is impeded.

Your score: _____

Comments:

Source: Folse, K. S. (2006). *The art of teaching speaking: Research and pedagogy for the ESL/EFL class-room.* Ann Arbor: University of Michigan Press, p. 222.

Administrative Issues for Assessing Speaking

Oral exams have to be scheduled, rooms booked, and teachers ready to examine. Speaking tests can be conducted live or they can be recorded. Alternatively, students can be tested over the phone.

When students are tested individually or in small groups, teachers are concerned about what to do with the students in the classroom who are not being tested. In colleges and universities, they can be assigned work to do in the independent learning center or in the library. In public schools, teachers often resort to conducting speaking exams at the front of the class while other students work silently. This arrangement is not ideal as the student being tested becomes self conscious and nervous, and the teacher cannot concentrate fully on the speaking exam. Security is also a concern as students overhear exam content and thus have extra preparation time.

To assess students' speaking skills in the regular classroom, select two or three students each class period and focus on their speaking during class participation. If you do this regularly, you will be able to track students' progress throughout the course in a fairly stress-free environment.

Ten Things to Remember about Speaking Assessment

1. **Choose tasks that generate positive washback for teaching and learning.**
   Select speaking assessment tasks that have a positive effect on the teaching and learning process. These tasks should be as authentic as possible.

2. **Allow time for a warm-up.**
   A warm-up will probably improve results. Speaking tests can be traumatic for second language learners. Use a warm-up activity to put students at ease.

3. **Keep skill contamination in mind.**
   Don't give students lengthy written instructions that must be read and understood before speaking.

4. **Remember that larger samples of language are more reliable.**
   Make sure that students speak long enough on a variety of tasks. You must have enough material for an accurate assessment.

5. **Choose a range of appropriate techniques.**
   Use more than one activity during an oral exam, as this is more authentic. Multiple measures within an exam give more reliable results than a single activity.

6. **Ensure valid and reliable scoring by choosing an appropriate scale.**
   Decide with your colleagues which speaking skills are most important and adopt a grading scale that fits your program. Whether you adopt a holistic or analytical approach to grading, create a recording form that enables you to track students' production and later give feedback for improvement. Remember, you can use different forms of grading for different tasks.

7. **Train teachers in scoring.**
   Let's face it: some teachers are better than others in using a rating scale. Train teachers in scoring, and practice together using the scale until there is a high rate of inter-rater reliability. Conduct moderation or calibration sessions with high-stakes speaking exams.

8. **Try to personalize the test by using the students' names.**
   Address students by their name to personalize the test. If you make personal comments, do not monopolize the exam by talking too much.

9. **Carry out speaking assessments and oral exams in a suitable venue.**
   Whichever type of assessment you're doing, you will need a relatively quiet room with good acoustics. This is especially important if you want to record the assessment.

10. **Never mark the test in front of the students.**
    It is distracting for students to see teachers marking in front of them. The best solution is to have two teachers administer the oral assessment, one functioning as interlocutor and the other as assessor in the background. If you administer a speaking test alone, wait until students have left the room before you record their marks. If you must take notes during the exam, make sure you tell students beforehand that you'll be doing this.

Extension Activity

Mr. Knott just gave his speaking tests. Here is a transcript of his speaking test with David, a student in his third period class. Try to identify the four stages of a speaking test: warm up, level check, probe, and wind down.

Transcript of Mr. Knott Administering Speaking Test

Mr. Knott: Hello, David. Can you tell me your name, please?

David: My name is David Jones.

Mr. Knott: Do you live in Chicago?

David: Yes.

Mr. Knott: Do you have any pets?

David: No.

Mr. Knott: Okay, David, remember this is a speaking test. You've got to say more so I can give you a grade. Tell me about your family, your classes, and your hobbies.

David: Which one would you like me to start with?

Mr. Knott: Any one you like.

David: What were my options again?

Mr. Knott: Please talk about your hobbies.

David: One of the things I really like to do is travel during the summer vacation with my family. Last summer we went to Hawai. . . .

Mr. Knott: Hawaii . . . fabulous. I've been there three times, and each visit was better than the rest. My favorite place was Maui. The beaches were fantastic, and I even learned to scuba dive when I was there. Probably the greatest thing about Hawaii was the shopping, lovely weather, and great variety of things to do. You can visit Pearl Harbor and see the USS Arizona. What a sad sight that was. It's a great place even if you don't like the beach. We spent one day hiking up to the top of Diamond Head. Oh. . . . enough of that. Let's move on to the next part of your speaking test. Here is a picture of a classroom scene. Could you please describe it for me?

David: Ah . . . well. . . . The picture is really not very clear. I know it is a picture of a classroom, but that's all I can tell you about it.

Mr. Knott: Excellent, David. Now let's move on to the role play. I forgot to bring the cards, so I'm just going to explain the situation to you. I'm a patient who has just

suffered a heart attack. You are my surgeon. Our con-
versation will take place just after my triple bypass.
We are going to discuss my post-operative treatment
and rehabilitation. Are you ready???

David: *Ah. . . . I guess. . . .*

How would you rate Mr. Knott's first speaking exam? What feedback would you give him? Mr. Knott let Ms. Wright listen to his taped speaking test with David. Here is the feedback Ms. Wright gave him.

Transcript of Ms. Wright's Feedback to Mr. Knott

Ms. Wright: First of all, Mr. Knott, congratulations for surviving your first batch of speaking tests. How did you find the experience?

Mr. Knott: Thanks. To tell you the truth, I found it just as stressful as the students.

Ms. Wright: Well, that's only natural. Let me tell you the things I liked about this particular speaking test. The first thing was that you taped it. Recorded speaking tests are always useful because we can engage in activities like this one. Another thing I liked is that you started with a warm-up to try to relax David. The highlight of the interview was that you used a range of speaking tasks starting with a Q & A warm-up, moving on to a description of a picture, and then on to a role play.

Mr. Knott: Why thanks. . . . But if I did all the right things, why did David not respond well? He's one of my best students.

Ms. Wright: Well, Mr. Knott . . . to be honest. David did not really get a chance to speak, as you did most of the talking. If we listen to the part where you asked him about his hobbies, the minute he mentioned Hawaii, you went off on a two- to three-minute description of your trips there. Then when you saw that time was slipping away, you went immediately on to the picture description.

Mr. Knott: Oh, haha! I guess you're right.

Ms. Wright: In the warm-up, it was a good thing that you personalized the exam by calling your student by his first name, David, but then you followed up by asking him his name. Probably a different question like "How are you doing today?" would have been more effective. Then the rest of your questions were of the yes/no variety. These types of questions don't generate much

	discussion, as you found out. Your next question was a three-parter. It would have been better to ask these question one at a time.
Mr. Knott:	I guess my warm-up was a bit of a disaster! What about part two, the picture description?
Ms. Wright:	I really liked the task you chose, but as you yourself noted, the picture you used for the description was not clear. It's important that any time we use visuals that they be clear and reproduce well.
Mr. Knott:	Ok. Good point. How about the role play? I think that went well.
Ms. Wright:	Role plays are great for speaking tests, but next time remember to bring your cards. I also think it would have been better to choose a more authentic task. To have a student pretend to be a heart surgeon is already too difficult. It is far-fetched and I believe too advanced for this level. In keeping with your health theme, having David play a student and you play a counselor would have been more purposeful. All in all, Mr. Knott, you did a fine job for your first speaking exam. I think given the discussion we've just had that perhaps you should allow David to take the exam again.

7 Student Test-Taking Strategies

Although teaching and assessment differ, the cornerstone of validity ties them closely together: *Test what you teach and how you teach it.* In your instruction, strive to emphasize important objectives and demonstrate ways in which they could be assessed. Make sure students are familiar with all formats and rubrics that they will encounter in assessment situations, and encourage students to use them to develop review tests for each other. For writing assignments, make your scoring system clear and familiarize students with it through self- and peer assessment.

In today's universities, grades are substantially determined by test results. So much importance is placed on students' test results that often just the word *test* frightens students. The best way for students to overcome this fear or nervousness is to prepare themselves with test-taking strategies. This process should begin during the first week of each semester and continue throughout the school year. The key to successful test-taking lies in a student's ability to use time wisely and to develop practical study habits.

Effective Test-Taking Strategies

Effective test-taking strategies are synonymous with effective learning strategies. This section provides suggestions for long-term successful learning techniques and test-taking strategies, not quick tricks. There is nothing that can replace the development of good study skills.

Here are some of the things Ms. Wright does to help students approach tests with confidence. She encourages them to:

- make a semester study plan that includes assessment and due dates for assignments
- come to class regularly and immediately check on any missed work
- use good review techniques individually and in study groups
- organize pre-exam hours wisely, allowing time for both review and rest
- understand how to take different kinds of exams and practice these skills in the classroom under low-stakes conditions
- use strategies appropriate to the particular skill areas
- strategize an exam plan by planning for what will happen on exam day
- reflect on each assessment experience and regard it as part of learning
- build learner autonomy because students are acquiring life-long learning techniques and strategies, not just short-term ways to get through a particular exam or course

Make a Semester Study Plan

Students need to plan their study time for each week of their courses. They should make schedules for themselves and revise them when necessary. These schedules should:

- **Be realistic.** Keep a balance between classes and studying. Block out space for study time, class time, family time, and recreation time.

- **Include a study place.** Finding a good place to study will help students get started; don't forget to have all the materials needed (i.e., pens, paper, textbooks and reference books, highlighter pens, etc.).

- **Include a daily study time.** Students forget things almost at once after learning them, so they should immediately review materials learned in class. Students should go over the main points from each class and/or textbooks for a few minutes each night. Encourage students to do homework assignments during this time as a good way to remember important points made in class.

- **Allow plenty of preparation time for important assessments.** Teachers should provide students with as much advance notice as possible about upcoming tests and due dates for assessments such as projects and portfolios. Students can learn useful time management skills in breaking down their preparation for these major events into smaller steps such as submitting drafts, reviewing certain textbook units, or taking practice tests.

Attend Class Regularly

For language learning to take place, students need to come to class on a regular basis. It is not surprising that poor attendance correlates highly with poor test results. Teachers need to point out early in the semester what constitutes legitimate reasons to be absent and stress the advantages of regular attendance.

It is also important that students feel motivated to attend regularly and see that they are making progress. Learning a language is an uneven process with times of rapid development mixed with plateaus when students seem stuck at one level. Journals, vocabulary notebooks, reading rate charts, and portfolios provide positive evidence that students are indeed moving ahead. Encourage students to use such tools to monitor their own progress.

Use Good Review Techniques

If students make a semester study plan and follow it, preparing for exams should really be a matter of reviewing materials. Research shows that the time spent reviewing should be no more than 15 minutes for weekly quizzes, two to three hours for a midterm exam, and five to eight hours for a final exam.

When reviewing for a test, students should do the following:

- **Plan review sessions.** Review the course outline, notes, and textbooks and list the major topics. How much time was spent on each topic in class? Did the teacher note that some topics were more important than others? If so, these should be emphasized in review sessions.

- **Take a practice exam.** By taking a practice exam, students will have an idea of the tasks/activities that they will encounter on the actual exam and the point allocation for each section. This information can help them plan their time wisely. Increasingly, practice exams for major tests are available on the Internet. Print versions of practice exams are available in bookstores, including some of the large national chain book dealers. In addition, many textbook publishers have a student website to accompany the textbook that includes online practice tests and quizzes. Students can access these sites wherever they have an Internet connection. However, teachers should caution students not to practice the same exam repeatedly because the increase in their scores reflects familiarity with the exam (to the point of memorization), not increased skill mastery. If students will take a computed-based test (CBT), it is especially important that they take a tutorial before the actual exam so that they understand the features of the program such as scrolling reading passages, indicating answers, and navigating from one section to another.

- **Review with friends.** Studying with friends in a study group offers the advantage of sharing information with others reviewing the same material. Small groups work best so that each student has an opportunity and a group responsibility to actively participate. Some students thrive in study groups because they feel more comfortable talking with their peers than talking in class. Explaining something to other students in the group is often helpful in clarifying a process or content. A study group, however, should not take the place of studying individually.

Organize Pre-Exam Hours Wisely

Students who have regularly reviewed course materials throughout the semester don't have to cram at the last minute. They can concentrate their efforts on their particular areas of difficulty and conduct an overall review of the material to be tested.

Physical and mental fitness are important considerations for good test-taking. These can be best achieved with adequate rest and nutrition in the hours preceding the exam. A well-rested, well-fed student who has prepared thoroughly is likely to be calm and self-confident, two other important factors for successful test-taking. Some teachers have found it useful to encourage students in stress-reducing activities such as exercise or listening to music in the pre-exam period.

Become Familiar with Instructions and Formats

A recent research project investigating the reading skills of English students has shown that students frequently fail to read directions or read them superficially to save time. Teachers can help students be more successful on tests by familiarizing them with the language of rubrics or instructions, particularly the cue words or phrases commonly used to give directions for the tasks students encounter. For example, if an instruction says to select the *best* answer for a multiple choice question, it implies that several answers may be partially correct but that one is superior to the others. In the following item, all the answer options have the same general meaning, but option A, "watch," is a better choice than the others.

> My favorite television program comes on at nine. Do you want
> to _____ it with me?
>   A. watch
>   B. look
>   C. view
>   D. observe

Alert students to special formatted words such as **bold**, *italic*, or underlining because words treated this way are often especially important.

Students also need to understand exactly how they are supposed to answer the questions. If they are supposed to select an answer, make sure your instructions are clear about how they are to select it (e.g., *circle the letter of the best answer* or *answer in three words or fewer on the line below the question*). On some standardized tests, students are not allowed to mark the question paper and must indicate their answers on an answer sheet. If a scan or "bubble" sheet is used, make sure that students know how to fill it out, whether to use a pen or pencil (some scanners don't read pen marks), and to fully erase a changed answer. Point out that an optical scanner will read an incompletely erased mark as the answer and will not accept two answers for the same item.

The policy on guessing answers varies on different exams. In most classroom tests, all questions are scored and the student's grade is based on the percentage of correct answers. Under these circumstances, students should be encouraged to guess if they don't know an answer and to not leave any questions unanswered. The guess may result in the correct answer, but the students' chances are much improved if they learn to eliminate unlikely options. This works best with objective format items, but may also work with short answer formats. On some standardized tests, there is a penalty for guessing. Familiarize yourself with the guessing policy on exams your students take and give out accurate information about it.

As noted in previous chapters, teachers should ensure that students are familiar with all formats they will encounter on classroom or standardized tests. If similar formats do not appear in the textbooks or other teaching materials, introduce them within the context of teaching. Model how new formats work and then give students hands-on practice with them. Provide time for discussion and questions about the new formats and attempt to clear up any misunderstandings.

In the past, miscommunications between teachers and students sometimes prevented open discussion about how some common testing formats work. Teachers were reluctant to provide information as a matter of security and students' anxiety increased because they didn't understand how they would be tested. Transparency means that teachers have a responsibility to share what they know about formats. Student-designed tests or quizzes make students more aware of how items are written, resulting in greater ability to answer test items. It is neither difficult nor time-consuming to build such activities into class sessions. For instance, if the reading task is a scientific passage, ask students to mark up the text to focus on points tied directly to the lesson such as specific vocabulary or use of the passive voice. For vocabulary, students could devise a matching exercise with a list of synonyms. They could transform passive sentences to the active voice. In the process of developing items, students will hone their comprehension skills.

Use Strategies Appropriate to the Skill Area

Teachers should train students in effective strategies for the various skill areas to be tested. Important activities (i.e., like note-taking for listening and writing tasks) should be demonstrated to students during classroom activities. Some new test-preparation books emphasize general language skill-building instead of specifically focusing on how the skills are tested in a particular examination. For example, *The Michigan Guide to English for Academic Success and Better TOEFL® Test Scores* (Mazak, Zwier, & Stafford-Yilmaz, 2004) prepares students for the TOEFL® iBT exam by building academic skills in reading, listening, writing, and speaking, not just on tasks similar to the test. In listening, for example, subskills include focusing on main ideas and details, note-taking, and listening for inference.

Spend time analyzing the particular skills that your students will encounter on standardized exams and then build strategies for these skills as part of classroom instruction. For example, many tests use a sentence completion format where students have to select a multiple choice option to fill a gap. When you introduce new vocabulary that includes phrasal verbs, collocations, or idioms, point out that these words occur together and if one is missing, it is important to look at all of the words surrounding the gap before making an answer choice. Draw students' attention to markers such as *but, although, so,* and *therefore* so students become aware of the shifts in meaning that these words signal.

Alert students to the words in reading instructions that indicate what kind of reading they need to do in order to answer the questions. It is futile to spend a great deal of time on a close reading of a long passage if the task requires extracting specific details to transfer to a chart. On the other hand, instructions that include words such as *author's intention, opinion,* and *inference* indicate that students will have to do more than quickly skim or scan the text. In fact, they may have to read very carefully to detect information that is not actually written. Reading for main ideas is often signaled by instructions that refer to *best title, paragraph topic,* or *key words.* Make students aware that main idea questions can refer to the entire passage, a single paragraph, or to information contained within certain line numbers that are found in the margins of the reading. Students who are aware of these conventions will be much better prepared to demonstrate their reading skills on examinations.

When you consider the development of good test-taking skills as synonymous with good learning skills, it is easy to integrate them into your classes. Refer to the skills chapters of this book for suggestions on particular strategies to include in your teaching.

Strategize Your Exam Plan

An important factor in test-taking is planning for what will happen on exam day and not leaving anything to chance. This builds your students' confidence and reduces anxiety.

Mechanics

Students feel better prepared if they have the mechanical aspects of taking an exam well in hand. They should arrive early at the designated exam room and find a seat. All books and personal effects (with the exception of student ID cards and writing materials) should be left at the front of the room. Students should come prepared with several pens or pencils and an eraser.

As soon as the exams have been distributed and students have been told to start, the student should write his or her name and ID number on all pages of the exam.

Procedures

If one section is given first, such as the listening portion of English exams, the student should focus attention on this section. With any section of the exam, the student is well-advised to do an overview of the questions, their values, and the tasks required. At this point, students should determine if the exam must be done in order (i.e., listening first) or if they can skip around between sections. The latter is not possible on some standardized exams where students must complete one section before moving on to the next.

Time Management

An important consideration in effective test-taking is time management. When exams are prepared, review time is usually factored into the overall exam design. Students should be encouraged to allocate their time proportional to the value of each exam section and to allow time to review their work. Teachers or proctors can assist students with time management by alerting them to time remaining in the exam. Computer based tests (such as the TOEFL® iBT) often show a countdown of the remaining time. Students should be made aware of this feature during practice exams.

In timed exams, students need to pace themselves so they finish within the allotted time yet still have time for planning and review. If you give exams with separate timings for each skill, time management may be easier. Encourage students to continue the good habits you built in the classroom. For a writing exam, if you emphasized brainstorming and outlining as a way to organize ideas, set aside a few minutes for these tasks before starting the actual writing. In fact, for classroom exams, you can encourage this by allocating some of the grade to evidence of planning. Similarly, show you value editing by expecting that students will allow time to look through their writing before considering it done. Suggest that students reserve a few minutes at the end of a section to review their answers and make sure they haven't forgotten or overlooked something important—such as questions on the reverse side of the test paper!

Sometimes students get bogged down on items or tasks they cannot answer. Advise them to leave those areas and focus on the sections of the exam they can do. If they have time at the end, they can return to the incomplete items and attempt to answer them. Find out in advance if there are sections of computer-based exams where this can be done.

Learn from Each Exam Experience

Each test should be part of the overall learning experience. Review test results with students, noting both strengths and weaknesses. If possible, give students a feedback sheet they can use for remediation or improvement. This feedback sheet could include scores on each section of the exam, the student's mean or average score on the entire exam, and an indication of areas where the student did well (strengths) and areas for improvement (weaknesses). Some teachers provide specific suggestions for further practice. If a student experienced a problem as a direct result of a test-taking skill, point that out so it doesn't happen again. For example, if a student didn't read instructions or ran out of time before completing a section, provide some suggestions for not repeating the error. Each exam students take should help them do better on the next one.

Build Learner Autonomy through Self-Assessment

Students will not always have a teacher to guide them. As they progress through life, they will usually have to rely on their own assessments of what they know—and don't know. For example, a new driver won't schedule a license examination until there is some degree of confidence in passing it. An employee will approach her manager for a raise when she is quite certain that her self-assessment of abilities will meet with success. Teachers can promote learner autonomy through self-assessment.

Self-Assessment

Self-assessment plays a central role in student monitoring of progress in a language program. It refers to the student's evaluation of his or her own performance at various points in a course. An advantage of self-assessment is that student awareness of outcomes and progress is enhanced.

Oscarson (1989), a noted scholar in the field of self-assessment, gives five reasons that self-assessment can be beneficial to language learning. First, he stresses that self-assessment truly promotes learning. It gives learners training in evaluation, which results in benefits to the learning process. Second, it gives both students and teachers a raised level of awareness of perceived levels of abilities. Training in self-assessment, even in its simplest form like asking "What have I been learning?" encourages learners to look at course content in a more discerning way. Third, it is highly motivating in terms of goal orientation. Fourth, through the use of self-assessment methodologies, the range of assessment techniques is expanded in the classroom. As a result of using self-assessment, the learners broaden their range of experience within the realm of assessment. Fifth, by practicing self-assessment, the students participate in their own evaluation (Dickinson, 1987). In effect, they share the assessment workload with the teacher.

Self-Assessment Techniques and Procedures

Student Progress Cards

Oscarson (1984) describes student progress cards as simple self-assessment tools that have been used in a variety of educational settings around the world. Quite simply, student progress cards define short-term functional goals and group them together in graded blocks at various levels of difficulty. Both students and teachers can participate in this activity. The students can check off (in the student column) each language skill or activity that they are sure of performing successfully. The teacher can later check off (in the teacher column) the activity once the learner has mastered it. Here is a sample progress card for a four-skill travel project.

Objective	Student	Teacher
Read and understand texts on a travel theme		
Listen to and understand passages on a travel theme		
Talk about past and future trips or vacations		
Write an itinerary for an upcoming vacation		

Rating Scales, Checklists, and Questionnaires

With rating scales, checklists, and questionnaires, learners rate their perceived general language proficiency or ability level. They often use "ability statements" such as, *I can read and understand newspaper articles intended for native speakers of the language* (Oscarson, 1984).

Learner Diaries and Dialogue Journals

Learner diaries and dialogue journals have been proposed as one way of systematizing self-assessment for students. Learners are encouraged to write about what they learned, their perceived level of mastery over the course content, and what they plan to do with their acquired skills. These techniques are discussed in greater depth in Chapter 4.

Videotapes

Video can be exploited in a number of ways to encourage self-assessment in the classroom. For example, students can be videotaped or they can videotape each other and then assess their language skills. An obvious advantage of using video in self-assessment is that students can assess not only their communicative or language skills but their paralinguistic (i.e., body language) skills as well.

Student-Designed Tests

A novel approach within alternative assessment is to have students write tests on course material. This process results in greater learner awareness of course content, test formats, and test strategies. Student-designed tests are good practice and review activities that encourage students to take responsibility for their own learning.

Learner-Centered Assessment

In learner-centered assessment, students are actively involved in the process of assessment. For example, students can select the themes, formats, and marking schemes to be used. Involving learners in aspects of classroom testing reduces test anxiety and results in greater student motivation.

Ten Things to Remember about Student Test-Taking Skills

1. **Student test-taking skills are really good learning skills.**
   Think of teaching and testing working together to build better language skills. Remember, the washback from testing affects what and how your students study.

2. **Build skill strategies into your classroom teaching.**
   Of course, there are differences between what happens in the classroom and in the examination hall, but wherever possible, highlight skill strategies and allow time for regular practice.

3. **Spend time on reading and following instructions.**
   Reading and following instructions is a real-life skill, so time spent on understanding the language and expectations of instructions is valuable for your students.

4. **Familiarize your students with a wide range of formats.**
   Students should be acquainted with most standard formats, especially those they are likely to encounter on standardized exams. Introduce new formats and allow plenty of time for practice.

5. **Promote and reward good planning.**
   Foster a positive attitude toward planning by rewarding students who make an effort. In developing grading schemes for projects, for example, reward completion on time.

6. **Discuss and practice timing issues.**
   Under stress, many students lose track of time. Provide opportunities for practice in timed tasks so that students develop time management skills in a low-stress situation.

7. **Encourage a variety of review activities.**
   At first, students may need assistance in learning to review efficiently. Help students form study groups and, if possible, provide time, space, and materials to get them started. Build a classroom library of suitable review materials and provide a list of Internet resources.

8. **Remind students of the importance of rest, recreation, and diet in exam periods.**
   Point out that athletes don't stay up all night without food before an important competition. Well-prepared students sleep, eat, and exercise before important tests.

9. **Provide students with helpful feedback.**
   Model the importance of reflection about assessment by asking students to write their thoughts in a dialogue journal or discuss them in a brief meeting. Be supportive with suggestions for improvement.

10. **Actively encourage learner autonomy through self-assessment.**
    Regularly use self-assessment techniques to foster learner autonomy. Send students the message that you respect their ability to monitor their own progress.

Extension Activity

Read the transcript of Mr. Knott's conversation with his colleague, Ms. Lee, and identify differences in their opinions.

Transcript of Conversation about Test-Taking Skills

Ms. Lee: The big state exam is tomorrow. Are your students ready for it?

Mr. Knott: I guess so. I've given the practice exam five times in the last two weeks, and their scores have really improved. Each time, when I ask for the answers, more of them are right.

Ms. Lee: Oh, you gave the same practice exam five times? Tell me, did the students who still had wrong answers understand why?

Mr. Knott: Probably not. We didn't have time to talk about it. I just checked the answers. I usually don't like students to mark their own papers. I don't use peer grading either; it's a waste of time. I hear that you have students design their own tests. Is that true?

Ms. Lee: Yes, it is. I find it's a good way to get them to review, and at the same time, they really understand how tests work. Have you tried that?

Mr. Knott: That's not for me! I think the teacher should be in control all the time. The students' job is to memorize the material, just like I used to. Why, I'd cram all night and study right up to exam time. I usually forgot to eat breakfast, and one time I almost fainted. I think we coddle students too much these days. No one ever told me what an exam was going to be like or spent time teaching how to read the instructions. Look, in my way of thinking, an exam is just something to get through, then you forget it and move on to the next thing.

Ms. Lee: Ooooh. There's the bell. Time to go back to class.

Ms. Lee's Comments

Issue	Comment
Students took same practice exam five times	Gave students a false sense of confidence because of the improvement in their scores due to familiarity with answers, not improved skills.
Answers not discussed	Without discussion, students don't understand where they went wrong.
Doesn't believe in self-assessment or peer assessment	These forms of assessment build understanding of grading criteria and expectations along with awareness of own ability.
Student-designed tests	Useful for review of materials as well as greater understanding of formats and tasks; helps students identify important topics to review.
Emphasis on memorization	Although it might work for a content course, it is not appropriate for a skills-based communicative language course.
Cramming, lack of sleep and food	With good planning, cramming is not necessary, but food, rest, and exercise are.
No coverage of exam structure, formats, or instructions	If students are unprepared, their scores are not an accurate or reliable indicator of their ability.
No reflection	Mr. Knott sees exams apart from the rest of the teaching/learning process, not an integral part.
Washback	Negative attitudes toward exams influence learning.

8 Administering Assessment

When administering a test, teachers should give students every opportunity to do well. To accomplish this, a careful consideration of factors that may affect test results is important. Ms. Wright takes her responsibility as exam coordinator seriously. Here are the administrative procedures she uses.

- She makes sure all students know where to go for the exam, when to be there, and what materials they'll need.
- She has the cleaning staff set up the test room appropriately the night before.
- She requires all students to keep their belongings at the front of the room or under their desks.
- She has developed several test administration policies (i.e., make-ups, special needs accommodations, latecomers, etc.) and sticks to them.
- She numbers all papers and requires students to sign them out.
- She always has incident report forms nearby during exams.
- She has answer keys ready so that marking can begin immediately after the exam.
- With multi-skills tests, she starts with the listening as that part of the test must begin and end at the same time.
- She gives students information about remaining time.

Considerations Prior to Test Administration

Scheduling Tests

The first consideration is the actual test scheduling. Ideally, any assessment should be scheduled at a time that allows students to do their best work. Before scheduling a test, check that the date does not coincide with special events like assemblies, fire drills, or Sports Day. Some teachers like to schedule their tests on a day when they will be away so that their substitute can administer the test. This is not recommended for several reasons. First, if questions arise about the content, the substitute may not be able to answer them. Also, the presence of a stranger in the classroom might make students nervous and uncomfortable, thereby affecting their scores. Third, a substitute is not familiar with students in the class and therefore may not be aware of special circumstances such as those with disabilities who need accommodation.

Providing Information to Students

The teacher should be as transparent as possible regarding student assessment. Students need to know when exams are scheduled and policies about arriving and departing. They need clear information about what they may and may not bring into the exam such as food and drink, calculators, electronic translators, etc. If dictionaries are allowed, make sure all students have the same one, and check dictionaries for notes inside. Let students know your expectations for items they must provide, such as an ID card, pens, pencils, sharpeners, and erasers.

Academic Dishonesty

At the beginning of the semester or academic year, describe for your students acceptable and unacceptable academic behaviors. Because some students may not know what constitutes academic dishonesty, give examples of cheating, plagiarism, and impermissible collaboration. Explain that cheating will not be permitted, and discuss school policies, procedures, and penalties for academic dishonesty. Some institutions have documents that define cheating and plagiarism and require students to sign a statement that they have read and understood the material.

In some cultures, it is natural for friends to work together to help one another. Small group or pair work learning activities in the classroom may give students the impression that collaborative test-taking is also permitted. Carefully explain the difference between teaching and testing situations so that there is no room for misunderstanding. The consequences for cheating in many schools are severe.

Physical Setting

In general the setting of a test should provide an atmosphere that is conducive to student learning. Most of the time, we administer tests in our own classrooms. Ask students to move their desks apart as much as possible. The ideal seating is every other seat and every other row. The test room should be free from interruptions and background noise and have adequate ventilation and proper lighting. When students enter the test room, have them place personal belongings on the floor rather than on their desks or in empty seats. If needed, schedule an additional room for overflow and a proctor to administer the exam there.

Test Assembly

All tests should be professionally compiled. This means that they should be typed, well formatted, and free of typos. Only high-quality photocopies should be passed out to students. The test should be clearly identified by a cover page with the name of the test, the date it was given, version number (in the case of multiple versions), and the time allowed. If no cover page is used, this information should be given in the header or footer.

In addition to writing their names on the cover page, students should write their names on all pages of the test and answer sheet. This will make it easier to track student work should the exam paper become separated. In large testing circumstances, you may need to check ID cards for signature and picture to prevent ringers (people who substitute for legitimate test takers).

The test instructions should be clear and concise whether they are given orally or in writing. If you are giving oral instructions, read slowly and clearly, but do not add or elaborate on anything as this will disadvantage students in other classes. Consistency equals reliability. Read the instructions word for word; do not paraphrase or cut out things you think are unimportant. You might need to practice this beforehand. Announce how many pages the test has and whether or not the test is printed on both sides of the paper.

The test paper should provide students with general instructions for the exam as a whole and separate instructions for each test section. Some of the information that should be included is:

- what the task requires (including specific requirements such as the number of words to write)
- how to answer the questions
- where to answer the questions (on the question paper or on a separate sheet)
- how many points each section is worth
- how many points each question is worth
- how much time is allowed for each section

Standardize the instructions (sometimes called the *rubric*) so students are familiar with the wording. If there are separately timed sections, arrange the exam so that students must wait to turn a page to the next section. That makes it easier for teachers to monitor.

It is very important for reliability to have clear instructions for the teachers who proctor an examination that is given to multiple classes. When administering high-stakes exams, whether they are in a paper-pencil format or a computer-based format, it is crucial to strive for the consistent administration of exams. During exam administration, make sure that all groups or classes of students taking the exam have the same amount of time to complete it and receive the same instructions. Giving certain groups more time or more explicit instruction unfairly advantages that group of students and skews results. Instructions should be developed well in advance of test administration and distributed to all the proctors so they have time to read them and raise questions before the exam date. Here are some sample proctoring instructions.

English 3

Progress Test #A

September 21, 2006

Proctoring Instructions

1. The English 3 Progress Test 1 consists of four parts (grammar, vocabulary, reading, and writing) and it should be administered in that order. Please pay strict attention to the timings for each section. The time allowances are as follows:

Grammar:	15 minutes
Vocabulary:	10 minutes
Reading:	20 minutes
Writing:	20 minutes

Please write start and finish time for each section on the board. It's also a good idea to "remind" students at periodic intervals throughout the exam, like "15 minutes remaining" and "5 minutes remaining," etc.

2. Once the test has begun, do not admit any late students. These students should be directed to wait in the principal's office. Refer these students to the designated floater in your area.

3. In the event that students have questions throughout the exam, please refer them to the written instructions on the exam paper. However, if a student makes a truly insightful comment that may have implications for mass misunderstanding among students, please notify Ms. Wright, the exam coordinator, immediately. You will be notified if any announcements of clarification need to be made.

4. There should be no students in the halls during the course of the exams. However, if students finish the final section (the writing exam) early, they can be dismissed. Please tell them to leave the exam room and the building quietly and immediately.

At the end of each exam, collect papers promptly and count them to make sure that the number of papers equals the number of students. Hand the papers over to the floater so marking can begin.

Answer Sheets

Students can either record answers on the test paper itself or transfer them to an answer sheet. The latter is a better option as it will decrease the amount of time to mark the test. If you use answer sheets with your students, make sure you build in time for them to transfer their answers. If you use answer sheets for listening, ask students to wait until all the listening is over before they start to transfer their answers. If you use Optical Mark Reader (OMR) or "bubble" sheets, make sure that students understand how to use them well in advance of the examination. Review such details as shading the box completely, checking to see if the question number matches the number on the OMR sheet, or thoroughly erasing changed answers so no dark fill remains.

Supplies

To prevent disasters, prepare your test materials well in advance. If by chance you spot a last-minute typo or problem with a question, inform students immediately. If you are doing a listening or speaking test that requires specialized equipment, check the equipment beforehand. Have extra supplies such as pens, pencils, and scratch paper on hand for students who have forgotten theirs. It is also useful to have a pencil sharpener. Sometimes students detach their papers while taking a test, so have a stapler in the room to reassemble test papers. Don't forget to have tissues on hand, too.

If you are administering a listening exam, have a tape script ready in case of power failure or equipment malfunction. Have a few extra copies of the exam in case students discover missing pages or pages that did not reproduce well. If the exam is given to several classes at the same time, have a "HELP!" card that the proctor can put on the hall door in case of problems or emergencies.

Test Administration

Time

Tell students how long they have at the beginning of the test, and give them time announcements throughout the exam to help them budget their time more effectively. With classroom tests, you generally have more flexibility with starting and ending times. However, on formal standardized tests, you must stick closely to the time allotted. At the end of the test, collect papers promptly so that certain students don't get extra time.

While collecting papers, check that each student's paper is filled out correctly: name on all pages of test paper, all sections of the test completed, and all parts of the test present. Make notes of any irregularities.

Administrator's Role

It is recommended that the test administrator (usually the teacher) maintain a friendly but stern demeanor. Make it known to students that you will not tolerate cheating or misbehavior during the test. If either occurs, issue warnings for misbehaving students and fill out an incident report.

Test Security

Maintaining security is important for any level of testing. When passing out papers, personally hand each student his or her own copy. Do not pass piles of test papers up and down rows. This practice encourages students to take an extra copy. Remind students about the test conditions. Rules that you might want to institute include no talking, no cell phone calls or text messaging, and the correct procedure for asking a question. Before the test begins, remind students of the penalty for cheating.

Once the exam starts, you (or a proctor) should remain in the room at all times. When proctoring, do not bring papers to grade or a novel to read, as your job is to periodically walk up and down the aisles to actively watch students. Spend some time stationed at the back of the room as students who are cheating will have to turn around in their seats to see where you are.

Students have developed clever ways of cheating during exams: using systems of hand and feet positions, tapping parts of their face to represent responses to multiple-choice questions, and loading tiny cassette recorders or iPods filled with test information. Our job as proctors is to stay one step ahead of students.

Let students know that you will be using computer programs and technology to detect cheating on essays or reports. Programs such as Turnitin and iThenticate compare students' responses and determine whether the information has been taken from Internet sources. Simply googling an essay or report will indicate if students have taken information verbatim from the Internet without properly citing it. Even if you do not actually use these techniques, telling students you might do it could prevent cheating.

Grading

After the test has been administered, teachers must mark the papers using the answer key prepared at the same time the test was developed. Make sure you can locate it quickly so that marking can commence in a timely manner. During marking sessions, mark only incorrect answers by indicating them with an X or a slash mark. (In EFL situations you might find yourself working with British teachers who have a different system of marking papers. They mark correct answers with a check mark and incorrect answers with an X.)

While grading, make sure that guidelines such as writing scales are readily available to the markers. Have a number of hand calculators available for tallying marks.

The most common grade system is the letter grade with A being the highest grade, then B, C, D, and F the lowest. Numerical grades are common, and they are usually expressed in percentage form. Often numerical percentage grades are translated into a letter grade. A third type of grading system is Pass/Fail. Some institutions use a new type of grading system called contract grading for which students agree to complete work at a certain standard for a set grade.

Grade Availability and Expectations

Inform students when their results will be available. In some situations, teachers are not allowed to release grades until the school administration approves them. If you work in this situation, make it clear that you must abide by the rules and cannot disclose student grades. Also inform students about your school's policy on challenging grades or asking for a review of the test paper. Stress the importance of fairness and accountability.

If you plan to use parts of a test again, it is important to keep it secure after it has been administered and graded. Let students know that they shouldn't expect to have their papers returned, and make sure that all teachers abide by the policy of keeping "live" tests secure.

Issues in Test Administration

Surprise Tests/Pop Quizzes

A good testing program does not have surprises. It should be transparent to all involved. Surprise tests or pop quizzes have no place in an assessment program as students have no chance to prepare for them. Students should always know when they are going to be tested, what they are going to be tested on, and how they will be tested. Never administer tests or quizzes as punishment or to discipline unruly students.

Some teachers feel that pop quizzes keep students on their toes. If you decide to use them periodically, make sure the weighting is not too heavy.

Latecomers

Students who arrive late for the test should not be allowed to take it. You should inform them of the date and time of the make-up exam if applicable and send them to the principal's or college administrator's office to wait out the exam. If you do not do this, the latecomer who is allowed to take the exam and who does poorly could complain that his or her tardiness affected the grade.

Incident Reports

A mechanism should be in place to record and report unusual behaviour or events that occur during a test administration. Hang a "Test in Progress" sign on your door to prevent needless interruptions.

Accommodations Policy

Make sure you have an accommodations policy for students who have medical problems or are physically challenged.

Ten Things to Remember about Administering Assessment

1. **Create a positive attitude toward testing.**
   Use tests to motivate your students by convincing them that their test results will be used to help them learn.

2. **Be transparent.**
   Explain the test purpose to students and what the test results will be used for.

3. **Follow proctoring instructions or instructions in the test manual to the letter.**
   Many teachers wonder why test developers are so detailed with their instructions. For results to be interpreted meaningfully, a test must be administered under standard conditions.

4. **Prepare policies and procedures well in advance.**
   Make sure that everyone involved in test administration is aware of policies and procedures. Questions or concerns should be raised at a time apart from test administration.

5. **Explain to students the distinction between teaching versus testing.**
   Although in teaching we recognize the importance of working in pairs or groups, in testing, our goal is to assess individual performance.

6. **Refrain from helping students who are having difficulty.**
   As teachers, it is natural to want to help students who are having a difficult time. However, this is unfair to those students who have prepared sufficiently. Resist the urge to help students and do not give hints.

7. **Note unexpected events that might interfere with assessments.**
   Fire drills, assemblies, and shortages of test papers are examples of incidents that should be noted, reported, and taken into consideration when interpreting test information.

8. **Adopt a specials needs assessment policy.**
   Make sure you have an accommodations policy in place for students who have specials needs.

9. **Inform students of the consequences of academic dishonesty.**
   Explain how cheating harms students and describe your institution's policy on academic dishonesty.

10. **Minimize the opportunities for cheating and plagiarism.**
    Make sure you are vigilant during test administration sessions.

Extension Activity

After the administration of the English 3 Progress Test, one of Ms. Wright's responsibilities as exam coordinator is to go through incident reports and make decisions about what actions (if any) should be taken. There were a number of potentially problematic incidents that took place in Mr. Knott's classes. Read the description of the incidents and think about what you would do. Then, find out what Ms. Wright recommends.

Incident 1:   *Five students in the class missed the test because of a previously scheduled sports event.*

Incident 2:   *Upon collection of the test papers at the end of the exam, two copies were missing.*

Incident 3:   *One of the other teachers reported that during the test, Mr. Knott walked up and down the aisles listening to his iPod.*

Incident 4:   *During the marking session, it was found that two students had exactly the same answers on the test. One of those students was among the strongest in the class; the other was among the weakest.*

Incident 5:   *Essays in Mr. Knott's second class of the day were much better than those in his first period of the day.*

Ms. Wright Responds:

Incident 1:   *Five students in the class missed the test because of a previously scheduled sporting event.*

Those five students should be allowed to make up the test. Before scheduling any assessment, the teacher should check with the students and school administrators to see if there are any conflicts.

Incident 2:   *Upon collection of the test papers at the end of the exam, two copies were missing.*

Mr. Knott needs to have better security procedures in place. I recommend that he number each test paper and pass out the exams in numerical order. That way if one copy goes missing, he'll know which student has it. This incident is disappointing as it means that this test will no longer be usable. We'll have to retire it.

Incident 3:   *One of the other teachers reported that during the test, Mr. Knott walked up and down the aisles listening to his iPod.*

Mr. Knott was only doing half his job. It was good that he actively walked around, but he needed to listen to what was going on in the exam session.

Incident 4:   *During the marking session, it was found that two students had exactly the same answers on the test. One of those students was among the strongest in the class; the other was among the weakest.*

Since no suspected cheating incident report was filed, there isn't much we can do about this. I'd recommend alerting the two students that you know something strange went on. The next time an exam takes place, separate these students and keep an eye on them, especially the weak student.

Incident 5:   *Essays in Mr. Knott's second class of the day were much better than those in his first period of the day.*

Classes meeting during the second half of the day were supposed to use Version B of the exam with a different writing task. Since Mr. Knott gave the same version to both his classes, there is not much we can do about this. This is certainly not the students' fault. It is only natural for them to discuss the test with their peers.

9 Using Assessment

The most frequently ignored phases of the assessment cycle are analysis, feedback, and reflection. Consequently, teachers don't obtain full information value from tests, and students miss out on adequate feedback for improvement. This chapter introduces basic analysis concepts and feedback techniques.

Like many busy teachers, Ms. Wright used to think that analysis was a waste of valuable time. As long as she got assessments graded and marks submitted to the school administration on time, she felt she had done her job. Besides, she thought that analysis required math skills she lacked. After agonizing through statistics in her education major, she vowed to steer clear thereafter. Then she attended a professional development workshop in which the presenters made a good case for doing analysis. Now she routinely:

- looks at the overall distribution of scores from every assessment
- plots grades on a simple histogram to help visualize the distribution
- checks the distribution against her expectations for that type of assessment
- uses the distribution to make final decisions about cut points
- conducts item analysis for representative items and those with problems
- earmarks problem items for reworking or discards them
- chooses well-performing items to recycle on future tests
- channels her analysis into useful feedback to students and administration

- shares her analysis results with her colleagues to inform teaching decisions
- suggests changes to the English program based on analysis data

You may think that Ms. Wright is a bit too enthusiastic about analysis and feedback. Why should anyone go to all that effort? After all, analysis and feedback still takes time that Ms. Wright could use for other purposes. The answer is that the payoff is really important. If we invest large amounts of time designing specifications, constructing and vetting good items, engaging in modcration sessions for reliable grading, and spending hours marking and figuring out grades, a little more investment will make the rest of our work pay off.

Teachers have an ethical responsibility to do analysis. High-stakes exams such as statewide standardized assessments and final course exams have a real impact on our students' lives. In the United States, there is a trend toward not awarding a full high school diploma to students who fail the statewide test, something that can affect lifelong chances for employment and further education. Students who fare poorly on important exams may spend a great deal of time and money in remedial programs until they pass required tests. Analysis provides a basis for accountability about the quality of an assessment. We cannot tell that a test or other assessment is really valid and reliable until we conduct analysis.

Analysis can provide very useful information about these things, among others:

- the proficiency of individual students
- abilities of all students in a class
- achievement of course goals by all students at a particular level
- quality of teaching
- how well course materials and teaching activities have helped students learn
- if an assessment reflected course aims and outcomes
- how well students at one school performed in comparison to another
- how reliable a test is and whether we can depend on the results
- whether an assessment distinguished between more and less able students

Simple analysis can be done by anyone with a calculator, pencil, and paper. Teachers like Ms. Wright who are a bit math-phobic should be assured that they do not need to remember or use formulas anymore because now there are economical and accessible computer programs for more complex analysis. Professional testers who work for large testing organizations use sophisticated analyses to thoroughly analyze their tests. Here, however, the focus is on simple analysis as a tool for the classroom teacher.

As useful as data from analysis are, raw statistics do not tell a story by themselves. You need to understand what the figures mean so that you can interpret them correctly. A teacher's experience and common sense are important elements in interpretation. A brief review of some basic concepts will help teachers interpret test results with more confidence.

Looking at the Whole Assessment

Distributions and Frequencies

One of the most important things to know about results from an assessment is how the students' scores are distributed. Are they all spread out, or do they cluster at certain points? You can start to see the distribution with a *frequency table*. Make a list of all the scores for an assessment in numerical order from lowest to highest. Then, write the number of students who got that grade next to the score. This spread of scores is called *dispersion*. You may already see some patterns, but a few simple statistics will help you understand more about your students' performance.

Frequency Table for Class B

score	frequency
68	1
65	1
64	2
63	3
62	3
61	2
60	2
59	1

Measures of Central Tendency

In statistics, the three ways to measure the middle of a distribution are called *measures of central tendency*. The *mean* is the arithmetic average, obtained by taking the sum or total of all the scores divided by the number of scores. This gives you information about how the average student did on the assessment. If this figure is very low, it may indicate that overall, students found the assessment difficult. This happens when the assessment is not well matched to the level of the students, when it is beyond their abilities, or when there are many flaws in the construction of a test. If you think the latter is the case, it would be important to do analysis on individual sections and items within the exam.

On the other hand, what does it mean if the average is very high? It could mean that the assessment wasn't challenging enough for the students' abilities or that it focused on tasks and content they already controlled. In the case of "mastery tests," that would be a good sign. If you were teaching an English for Specific Purposes (ESP) course for surgeons or airline pilots, you would certainly want everyone to score very highly. In general, though, a high mean may indicate that the assessment doesn't discriminate enough between students with different abilities and skill levels.

Mean scores can be computed for the test as a whole or for each section (i.e., listening, reading, writing etc.) of a test. Computing a mean score can give you information as to the reliability of the test. In general, mean scores that fall within the 70th percentile (i.e., from 70 to 79) are said to be valid indicators of test reliability.

Useful as the mean is, it can be misleading because it can be influenced by extremely high or low scores, sometimes called *outliers*. If you examine your frequency table and see scores at either extreme, then you might want to use one of the other two measures of central tendency. The *mode* is the most frequently occurring score, and the *median* is the midpoint score when you range all the individual scores from top to bottom. It is useful to use all three of these measures when you are trying to establish cut points for pass/fail or particular grade allocations.

Pass Rates

Once you have decided which scores equate to categories such as letter grades, you can compute the pass or failure rate for a given test or quiz by doing a grade breakdown. The first step in this process is to count the number of As, Bs, Cs, and Ds received on a given test. This number represents the pass rate. Divide this number by the total number of students who took the test, and you have the pass rate. To compute the failure rate, count the number of Fs or failing grades and divide this number by the total number of students who took the exam. Administrators often ask for pass rates for important assessments.

Histograms

Histograms, a type of bar chart, are visual representations of how well a group of students did on a test or quiz. Histograms can be easily drawn from a list of grade breakdowns (number of A, B, C, D, and F grades received on a test) or from the actual scores as shown on your frequency table. These totals are then graphed on a chart. The resulting pattern or curve represents how the class did as a whole on a test. Different kinds of tests produce differently shaped histograms. Norm-referenced proficiency tests (NRTs) in which students' scores are compared to other students in a large, normative group yield a broad spread of scores with a clump in the middle and "tails" at either end. This shape is often referred to as a *bell curve,* and it shows a normal distribution of student scores. On the other hand, criterion-referenced tests (CRTs) have a much narrower range of scores because they focus on the students' attainment of certain criteria such as course outcomes.

Standard Deviation

Standard deviation (SD) is another useful tool in analyzing assessment. This statistic gives us an idea of how closely scores are distributed around the mean. As previously noted, the mean can be easily influenced by high or low scores, so sets of scores could yield the same mean although their actual spread or distribution is very different. For example, Ms. Wright's classes might have the same mean because in one section most of the students scored in a cluster around the mean while in the other they were widely spread out from very low to very high. For example, here are two sets of scores for different classes, each with 15 students. In the first class, Class A, the scores were: 15, 23, 42, 55, 59, 63, 64, 67, 69, 72, 73, 75, 81, 84, and 96. For the second class, look at the frequency table on page 160. Both classes had a mean of 62.5 percent, but the distribution of scores around that mean is very different. The scores for the first class are widely spread out throughout the range while those for the second class are tightly clustered around the mean. The second class appears to be quite homogeneous while the first class is probably multi-level. The standard deviation tells Ms. Wright that the distribution of these classes is quite different, and she might want to consider why. One reason for a wide SD might be that a school cannot offer all the levels of language that students need, so instead they collapse levels.

Therefore, the students who "place" into a level might have widely varying levels of language. Standard deviation is supplied with analysis software or obtainable from many hand calculators.

Focus on Test Items

The old saying that the whole is greater than the sum of the parts is certainly true about assessment, but it is equally true that all the component parts need to do their part to make the overall test work. Classroom teachers use item analysis to check that individual items are working properly. Given the amount of work in designing good test items, many institutions recycle good items in a test bank. After the first time an item is used, analysis is done to see how the item functions within the test, including a careful analysis that the distractors are working as they should. If all is well, the item or set of items is kept secure and used again in future tests.

Faulty items also need item analysis to understand why they aren't working well. While grading, you may notice that many students got certain items wrong. This could be because of any of the item violations described in detail in Chapter 2, or it could happen because of unexpected interpretations of the question or distractors. Item statistics and analysis will help solve the mystery.

Item Difficulty

At the item level, the main analytical tool is *item difficulty*, sometimes called *facility value*. Both terms indicate the proportion of correct responses, which is figured by dividing the number of students who answered correctly by the number of students who attempted to answer the item. Item difficulty can range from high values such as .95 to low ones in the range of .15. Easy items found at the beginning of a test to ease students' anxiety often have an item difficulty of .85 or above. By contrast, items with a facility value of .15 are quite difficult because only a few students were able to answer correctly. As noted on page 37, ideal tests contain items at a mix of difficulty levels, so facility value is a good way of determining the level of particular items for classroom tests.

Item Discrimination

A second way of analyzing items is to compare how students did on a single item as contrasted to their overall performance on the entire assessment. This is called *item discrimination* because it examines whether the item distinguishes between stronger and weaker students. Remember, one purpose of assessment is to get information about students who are progressing and those who need further help, practice, or instruction. If both excellent and failing students answer a question correctly, the item does not discriminate and has a low value. On the other hand, items that do show differences between students are said to discriminate well and have higher levels such as .60 or more. Most items on a reliable test should discriminate at .30 or above.

To compute item discrimination, you have to divide the class into high and low groups, so once again the distribution comes into play. For this type of analysis, you will focus on the high and low groups and ignore the middle range. Divide the test population (i.e., the students who took the test) by four, according to their overall grades. In other words, in a class of 40, the 10 students with the top grades are in the high group and the 10 with the lowest scores are in the low group. For now, you don't need information about the middle 20 students.

For each item, count how many of the students in the high group got it correct and subtract the number of the students in the low group who got the right answer. Then divide that number by the group size, 10 in this case. That will give you the item discrimination. For example, if eight students in the high group answered correctly, but only three in the low group, the difference (five) divided by 10 would be .50. This would indicate that the item is discriminating well and thus contributing to the reliability of the exam.

Two points need to be made about item discrimination for classroom assessment. First, the procedure does not work well with small numbers, so if you have only one class with 25 students, it is not worth doing. However, if you have three sections of 35 students each, it is worthwhile. Second, occasionally you come up with a negative discrimination index that indicates more students in the low group answered correctly than those in the high group. This happens when stronger students over-interpret simple questions and assume that they are more complicated than they actually are. Clearly, those items need to be revised!

Distractors

For several types of objective tests where the answer is supplied, it is useful to see whether distractors are actually attracting students who do not know the correct answer. In the item writing phase, choose distractors that seem like plausible answers for someone who does not understand the point being tested. For example, for testing the main idea in reading paragraphs, the goal is to see if the student can separate levels of generality or specificity. Good distractors in a multiple choice item would include options that are both more general and more specific than the actual main idea at the paragraph level. One distractor might be a very general topic related to the passage as a whole while another might be a supporting detail from a specific example.

Distractor analysis is calculated by using the same high and low groups as in item discrimination. However, this time you want to create a table that shows how many students from each group were attracted to each distractor. If you find that some distractors don't attract any responses, then they should be changed. Look at those distractors that work for ideas about other options to replace the non-functioning distractors. As with item discrimination, some distractors attract students in the high group. Analyze them carefully to understand why they might have chosen the wrong answer. Their mistake may give you insight into problems with materials, instruction, or fossilization, a situation where students revert to something they learned earlier.

Here is the analysis of two items from a multiple choice reading task given to 1,400 students. What comments could be made about them?

Analysis of Two Items

Item 1

Item Difficulty	Discrimination Index	MCQ Option	Total % Responses	% Low Responses	% High Responses
.92	.15	a	.03	.07	.00
		b	.04	.08	.02
		c	.00	.00	.00
		d* (key)	.92	.83	.98

Item 2

Item Difficulty	Discrimination Index	MCQ Option	Total % Responses	% Low Responses	% High Responses
.41	.35	a	.33	.33	.33
		b	.08	.13	.03
		c* (key)	.41	.26	.61
		d	.17	.26	.04

The first item has an item difficulty of .92, so most students found it quite easy. In fact, it did not discriminate well between the high and low groups of students. Almost all (98%) of the high group identified the answer as option d, but so did 83 percent of the low group. No one chose distractor c, so it was not effective. It should be noted that this was the first item on the exam, so it functioned as a warm-up item in that position.

The second item has an item difficulty of .41, so many more students found it difficult. However the discrimination index is .35, so it did show a difference between weak and strong students, especially in the responses to the key, option c. In contrast to the first item, all distractors work in this item. Note that option a, an incorrect response, attracted as many students in the high group as in the low group.

Analysis Software

Teachers who have special responsibility for assessment may want to explore software that makes the process of analysis far easier and quicker. J. D. Brown (2005) offers clear guidance in using Microsoft's® Excel spreadsheet program to analyze and interpret test data. Hughes (2003) offers analysis software through his book's website. Many colleges and universities use Iteman commercial software; visit *www.assess.com/Software/iteman.htm* to see samples of item analysis and demonstrations of how the software works.

Whether you analyze with paper, pencil, and calculator or use special software, interpretation is a matter of thinking beyond the numbers. Experienced teachers have a well-developed sense of what to expect from their students. When your analysis produces unexpected results, persist in exploring the reason for the discrepancy. Instances of odd results often give us insight into how our students process language or take exams. Once we understand what happened, we can use those insights in our classrooms to improve instruction or exams.

Feedback

Recall from the circle diagram in Chapter 1 that analysis, feedback, and reflection are important parts of the teaching/learning cycle. By now, it is clear that assessment doesn't end when the grades are in. Analysis takes time and effort, but once the benefits are clear, administrators often support analysis because it provides them with useful information.

After conducting analysis, the next step is to interpret the results for stakeholders such as students, colleagues, and administration. Feedback can take many forms, from conferences and meetings to large reports and presentations. The crucial thing is to provide timely information, especially if the feedback concerns formative assessment. People have a tendency to regard feedback negatively, so counter this by including positive information. Your analysis will have shown many areas of improvement and progress, and it is important to emphasize what has gone well. Start with several positive statements to create a receptive response.

Carefully consider the people who will receive feedback and how they process information. We assume that students understand the copious information we provide on course outcomes or requirements for graduation, but often they do not. Effective feedback provides just the right amount of information in a usable form. If you schedule meetings with students, also provide a handout they can take away. It might summarize their main areas of strength and those that need improvement. Provide links to resources they can access to improve their skills and have a follow-up mechanism to see if they need further support. Turn feedback into positive washback by demonstrating to students that assessment is part of their learning.

When you meet with your colleagues, be sensitive to their concerns about their own teaching and the progress of their students. Point out that assessment is a group endeavor and that maintaining high standards is a shared responsibility. Be specific about points that need improvement, but don't get mired in details. Above all, let your colleagues know that you value their experience and judgment. Strive to make assessment inclusive instead of exclusive and provide constructive suggestions.

Administrators are often receptive to booklets or PowerPoint presentations that feature graphics, especially if you provide these in forms they can use themselves. However, keep in mind that statistics and graphics by themselves are just numbers and pictures. It is up to you to provide interpretation about what the figures and histograms mean.

The final step of reflection often occurs more than one time. Just after a major assessment, make notes of things that might be forgotten. Keep a small notebook or a computer folder just for this purpose. Similarly, during the analysis or feedback phases of assessment, keep track of things you would like to change or do differently. Over time, reflect, discuss, and experiment. In the end, every assessment is an opportunity for growth.

Ten Things to Remember about Feedback

1. **Make it timely.**
   Stale information is not very useful, so prioritize prompt feedback.

2. **Accentuate the positive.**
   Comment on progress and achievement. Start feedback with what was successful.

3. **Keep the end user in mind.**
   Think about the appropriate level of language and amount of information.

4. **Whenever possible, use graphics to make your point.**
   It's true about pictures being worth many words.

5. **Be specific, but don't get bogged down in details.**
   Support your interpretations with details but avoid technicalities.

6. **Clearly identify areas for further development.**
   After formative assessment, make constructive suggestions for immediate improvement.

7. **Keep the course outcomes in mind.**
   In your feedback, use your analysis to show whether students are meeting course outcomes. If there are problems, provide suggestions for improvements.

8. **Trust teachers' experience and judgment.**
   Statistics require expert interpretation to be meaningful.

9. **View feedback as a vehicle for transparency and accountability.**
   Encourage openness. Feedback is an opportunity to raise awareness of how assessment works.

10. **Turn feedback into washback.**
    Informative and timely feedback creates a sense that assessment really is useful.

Extension Activity

On pages 160 and 162, sets of scores were given for two classes. What would these scores mean if they were for one of Mr. Knott's classes at two different times?

Mr. Knott's

Mr. Knott has just started to analyze items on his midterm exam. Here are item analyses for two MCQ reading items with four options each. What kind of feedback would you give to him?

Item 3

Item Difficulty	Discrimination Index	MCQ Option	Total % Responses	% Low Responses	% High Responses
.77	.39	a	.13	.21	.03
		b	.01	.00	.01
		c	.10	.20	.01
		d* (key)	.76	.57	.95

Item 4

Item Difficulty	Discrimination Index	MCQ Option	Total % Responses	% Low Responses	% High Responses
.48	.61	a	.40	.57	.24
		b* (key)	.48	.22	.73
		c*	.04	.07	.01
		d	.07	.13	.02

Here are some things on which you might want to give feedback:

On the whole, are these good items? Why or why not?

In what ways could these items be improved?

Do you think Mr. Knott should use these items in his item bank? Explain.

MEMO

To: Mr. Knott
From: Mr. Lee
Subj: Analysis

First, congratulations on putting information from the testing workshops into practice! Your colleagues understand that so many aspects of assessment are confusing at first, but we hope that by holding workshops and providing support to each other we can raise standards throughout the department. It's clear that you are learning a lot.

Here are a few comments on the questions raised in the extension activity:

1. What could two such different sets of scores for one class mean?

It is possible that the widely distributed set of scores came from a proficiency test that we used for placement at the start of the school year. Your students came into the high school from a variety of previous educational experiences. Some were promoted from middle schools within the school system where they had special instruction as English Language Learners (ELLs). Others came from bilingual private schools or public schools in other states. In one case, a student was home-schooled and in another case, the student was a recently arrived immigrant with very little previous study in English. At the beginning of the year, before you provided any instruction, there was a wide range of English ability.

Now at the end of a year's instruction, the more concentrated scores represent the achievement of the class on material that has been taught. The scores fall in a narrow range around the pass mark of 60 percent. It is evident that some students have really improved enormously, but I can imagine that you are worried about what happened to the students whose marks seem to have declined. I'd like to remind you that the second of these two assessments focuses on writing and speaking instead of the receptive skills and that you are paying more attention to accuracy than fluency. That could account for some of the differences.

2. Item analysis

On the whole, these are both good items and you should consider recycling them after you have made some changes. Item 3 is moderately easy with an item difficulty of .77, but it does in fact discriminate between the groups of students. However, did you notice that option B is not attracting many students? You will want to replace that distractor with one that works for you. To get an idea of what might be a good replacement, look at options A and C and consider why students in the low group are attracted to those responses.

Item 4 is much more difficult with an item difficulty of .48. Remember that you want a range of item difficulty levels in your exams, so you may find this to be a good model for a midrange item for the kinds of students in our program. It discriminates well with an index of .61, but the true story is clearer when we look at which answer options really distract students. Even with a relatively challenging item, 73 percent of the high group chose the key, but a quarter of even that group was attracted to option A. The low group was really distracted by option A with 57 percent selecting it. We see this kind of distribution with grammar items when they test a point that students learn late, such as third person "s" on present tense verbs or the appropriate use of articles. We also see this with forms that students learned early in their exposure to English that have become "fossilized" through repeated use without correction.

I hope these comments help you to see that analysis can give us useful insights about the process of language learning.

Assessing ESL Students' Knowledge of Content in K–12 Classes

10

As the title of this chapter clearly indicates, this information is for K–12 teachers. K–12 teachers have a myriad of daily challenges, including how to teach content such as science, reading, or math to a student whose English ability is limited. There are no easy answers, but the information in this chapter will help teachers better serve their ELLs.

Ms. Wright is one of thousands of elementary, middle, and secondary school teachers who are responsible for students' progress in math, science, history, and English. More and more, Ms. Wright has seen an increase in the number of her students whose first language is not English. A certain percentage of these students speak English well enough to function successfully in school. However, many of these English language learners (ELLs) do not have sufficient English language ability to demonstrate their knowledge in subject areas even when they have understood and mastered the content material.

Ms. Wright is aware of the plight of these students. She has received additional training in second language acquisition and ESL problems. To help ELLs, she

- is aware of the state-approved (in this case, Florida) testing accommodations, e.g., allowing extra time or a bilingual dictionary
- appreciates the important role that ELLs' limited vocabulary ability has on learning and, as a result, on assessment
- teaches key vocabulary in her lessons to minimize its negative impact in assessing content
- uses many types of questions on her assessments, including

objective (which are not language demanding) and extended
answer (which are language demanding)

- allows for alternative assessments that are not so language
demanding, e.g., a science project

As the number of non-native speakers in English-speaking countries contin-
ues to rise, so does the number of non-native students in regular K–12 classrooms. As U.S. Secretary of Education Margaret Spellings noted in a 2005
speech, "English language learners (ELLs) are the fastest-growing student population in America. Today, one out of every nine students is learning English as a
second language. That's about 5.4 million children—almost the population of
Arizona, or Maryland, or Tennessee. Their numbers will more than double in
the next 20 years. By 2025, English language learners will make up one out of
every four students in our classrooms." Despite this growing number of
non–native-speaking students, the vast majority of classroom teachers have little or no training in teaching and assessing non–native-speaking students in traditional content areas such as math or science. The result is often ineffective
teaching, which is then compounded by inappropriate or even incorrect assessment practices.

Florida is a good example of a state that has had to grapple with a large
number of non-native students in its schools (Folse & Brummett, 2006). With
approximately 300,000 non-native English–speaking students (MacDonald,
2004), schools in Florida face a shortage of qualified teachers who are knowl-
edgeable about key issues in second language learning and thus able to educate
this group of Limited English Proficient (LEP) students effectively (Stebbins,
2002). Resulting from a lawsuit two decades ago, the 1990 Consent Decree
between the League of United Latin American Citizens (LULAC) and the
Florida Department of Education requires that all LEP students receive equal
access to programming that is appropriate to their level of English proficiency.
Thus, teachers have to modify their instruction and assessment to cope with
these challenged learners. In addition, assessment has taken on an even greater
role from the No Child Left Behind Act, which mandates that students be
retained or kept back from progressing to the next grade if they do not satisfy
state-established norms, often measured in objective examinations.

Exactly how serious is the situation for LEP students in Florida? In 2001,
the retention rate for secondary level (grades 7–12) ELLs in Florida was an
astonishing 18.2 percent, one of the highest rates in the entire nation (Kindler,
2002). In comparison, the state of Texas, which also has a very large population
of ELLs, had a retention rate of 10.4 percent, which is about 43 percent less
than that of Florida.

These few statistics indicate the clear gravity of the problem in K–12 class-rooms in the United States. Teachers need to understand how their evaluation methods coupled with their students' low English proficiency combine to impact assessment marks. While the previous chapters in this book have addressed constructing different types of questions or testing a specific language skill, Chapter 10 deals with assessing non-native speakers in K-12 content classes such as mathematics or science. This chapter identifies some of the threats to good assessment for ELLs as well as recommends specific actions that K–12 teachers can easily undertake to assess ELLs more accurately.

The Example of Mathematics

It is often said that of all the school subjects, mathematics is the one in which non-native speakers should do best, not because they are somehow inherently good in math, but rather because numbers do not impose the linguistic demands that prose-based subjects such as reading/literature, social studies, or history do. While it is true that the pure study of just numbers may require fewer words than in the case of, say, literature, learning math instruction does require a great deal of language knowledge. In sum, math is not just numbers.

We will discuss math assessment issues from two angles: class content and student background. For class content, we discuss word problems, one of the most common assessments used in math. For student background, we discuss how ELLs may have been taught math differently depending on their country of origin and how this different training may impact assessment in K–12 in the United States.

Word Problems

It is impossible to imagine a mathematics assessment that does not contain word problems. A word problem presents numbers within a real-world context. Instead of adding 4, 7, and 2, learners read statements about three situations. Consider these two examples:

Problem 1: $4 + 7 + 2 = \underline{\ ?\ }$

Problem 2: Susan read four books in May. In June, she read seven books. In August, however, she read only two books. How many books did she read all together?

Fourth graders who spoke very little English could answer Problem 1 because of two things: (1) they know the math and (2) they can read the question. In sharp contrast, problem 2 is unsolvable for the very same fourth graders—not because of a sudden decrease in math knowledge but rather because of language issues. It is easy to see that students do not know enough English to know *read* or *all together* or *the three months* and therefore not understand that they are supposed to add these numbers together. Moreover, since the numbers are represented by the words *four, seven*, and *two* instead of the numerals *4, 7*, and *2*, students cannot even take a guess as to what the answer might be. (If numerals were used in Problem 2, then students could guess that the answer might be 13 if they added, 56 if they multiplied, or even –1 if they subtracted. Only 13 would be correct, but at least the other guesses would be plausible.)

Clearly, the linguistic demands of word problems can impact assessment results in a math class, so should math teachers avoid word problems? Definitely not. On the contrary, word problems are a fundamental part of the math curriculum. If we look at a word problem in terms of Bloom's (1984) six levels of abstraction of questions, the purpose of word problems is to test not just knowledge or comprehension but application, analysis, synthesis, and even evaluation. Word problems are an integral component in U.S. math classes as the math curriculum seeks to produce learners who are able to do much more than mere rote memorization.

What is important is that teachers realize that ESL students may make mistakes with word problems when they do in fact know the underlying mathematical issues, which ironically was the purpose of asking the math question in the first place. One of the hallmarks of good assessment is that it should always match teaching. That is, you should test material the way it was taught. If the math problems were covered in class, then they should appear on the test in proportion to the amount of time they were covered in class.

In addition to regular classroom assessment, ELLs often do poorly on large-scale assessment examinations because unfamiliar language on the exams presents problems. Considering the example of Florida again, the Florida Comprehensive Assessment Test (FCAT) is a statewide assessment given to Florida students in Grades 3 through 12. In 2005, the mathematics section of the Grade 4 FCAT consisted of 40 multiple choice questions. Of these questions, none—not a single one—was expressed in the form of a simple math equation, as in 20 + 13 = _?_. In fact, of the 40 questions, 26 (65 percent) required students to solve the answer based on words and a visual (e.g., a map or geometric figure) or a table of data. The remaining 14 questions (35 percent) were word problems alone. While the curriculum demands that word problems be taught, they now receive even more emphasis in class because of the importance of this high-stakes examination for students whose futures depend on their scores, teachers whose pay and teacher effectiveness (and in some cases jobs) may be associated with students' scores, and school administrators whose jobs are connected to the overall grade that schools receive based on all students' scores in all subjects.

For all the reasons just outlined, you should not avoid word problems. Word problems are an integral part of the math curriculum. However, you should be aware of the vocabulary used in the problems. It is the math teacher's job to make sure all learners know the most commonly used words, especially verbs. As you consider the following ten word problem examples, can you identify one or two key vocabulary words that are necessary in your final determination as to whether to add, subtract, multiply, or divide?

Word Problem A:	Kevin has 5 baseballs. He gives away 2 of them to his cousin. How many baseballs does Kevin have now?
Word Problem B:	There are 6 tables with a total of 18 chairs around them. If each table has the same number of chairs, how many chairs are at each table?
Word Problem C:	A zoo has 7 male zebras and 9 female zebras. How many zebras are there in the zoo?
Word Problem D:	Rina wants to buy a new TV set that costs $240. She has $180 of her own money. If she borrows $50 from her aunt, will she have enough money to buy the TV set?
Word Problem E:	There are 4 salads on the table. Each salad has 4 cucumber slices and 2 cherry tomatoes. How many cherry tomatoes are there in all?
Word Problem F:	An aquarium contains 11 tropical fish. Right now 3 of them are stationary. How many fish in the aquarium are moving?
Word Problem G:	The 3 horses and 2 ponies in the stable need new horseshoes. How many horseshoes does the owner need to buy?
Word Problem H:	There are 5 cases of tennis balls. Each case holds 30 balls. How many tennis balls are in the cases?
Word Problem I:	The total prize money in yesterday's drawing was $25,000. The 5 winners shared the prize equally. How much money did each winner receive?
Word Problem J:	A magician begins his show with 9 rabbits and makes 1 disappear during the show. At the end of the show, how many rabbits are left?

The solution here is not to avoid word problems but rather to teach and assess key language, especially vocabulary, that is important in answering word problems. At first, this task may seem monumental because there are so many words in English. However, the words that are most commonly used are limited. Start by analyzing your math textbook. You might even have students help you to compile this list, perhaps as part of a regular assignment or for extra credit. Part of the battle in learning new words is getting students to become aware of words that they do not know since non-native speakers frequently overestimate their vocabulary knowledge (Folse, 2004).

Once you have compiled a list for your particular students' needs—which would include comprehending not only the textbook unit on fractions but also word problems in teacher-generated assessments and any standardized tests that ask about fractions—then you should make these words a part of your instruction for all students, both ELLs and native speakers. For example, take the word *over*. In fractions, you might use over meaning "above," as in 4/3 is read as 4 over 3. However, when you do the math procedure of converting the fraction 4/3 to a whole number, your answer is 1-1/3. In explaining this in English, you might say, "Class, first we divide 3 into 4 and that gives us the whole number 1, but we still have 1/3 left over." Here we have *over* meaning "extra." However, you should teach the expression *left over*, as in this math problem: *Susan had 87 cents. She bought a banana for 40 cents. How much money did she have left over?* The solution to math problems is to teach both the mathematical and language tools that students need to arrive at the correct solutions.

International Differences in Mathematics

Contrary to popular belief that math is internationally similar, mathematics does vary from country to country. If you are teaching very young children, they may not have had any schooling in another country, which means that these students will learn the math conventions taught in the United States alongside their English-speaking counterparts. However, older students are more likely to have been schooled in their home country. For these students who have been educated in other countries, previously studied mathematical conventions may be different and therefore a source of assessment error. The chart provides examples of differences in the form of the numbers, the use of decimals, and the method of showing work.

Differences in Math across Countries

Difference	United States	Non-United States
Numbers	1 2 3 4 5 6 7 8 9 0	Arabic: ٩ ٨ ٧ ٦ ٥ ٤ ٣ ٢ ١ ٠ Chinese: 一 二 三 四 五 六 七 八 九 十
Decimals	point [.] for percentages; 82.5% or 5.1%	Comma widely used for percentages: 82,5% or 5,1%
Calculations	division is written with the divisor to the left of the dividend $$205$$ $$4\,)\,\overline{820}$$ $$\underline{8}$$ $$2$$ $$0$$ $$\underline{20}$$ $$\underline{\underline{20}}$$	Latin America: division is written with the divisor to the right of the dividend and the lines are different; the small ticks indicate that the numeral has been used already. $$8`2`0` \,\lfloor 4$$ $$= 20 \quad 205$$

Our recommendations for K–12 teachers here are two-fold. First, be aware that ELLs who have studied math in another country may be accustomed to a different math, ranging from the way the numbers are written to the way to solve a given problem. Second, help students notice these differences and understand that even though the methods of arriving at the answer may be different, the underlying mathematical concepts are the same.

The Example of Science

For ELLs, perhaps the most daunting aspect in science assessment is their low English proficiency, especially their limited vocabulary knowledge. ELLs' language deficiency impacts their ability to read and comprehend their science texts, which is further compounded by students' insufficient writing ability. This becomes obvious as students attempt to solve extended answer questions. (Note: Though this chapter discusses only mathematics and science, many of the assessment issues in science also occur in social studies and literature.)

Science classes and science textbooks contain two kinds of languages: general vocabulary and technical vocabulary. ELLs already have a lower level of general vocabulary knowledge than their native-speaking counterparts. In addition, even words that the ELLs already know can be problematic because many of the general vocabulary words have a different, very specialized meaning in the context of science. For example, a *base* in science is contrasted with an acid but means "foundation" in general English. A *table* with the elements is not the same as a table in the kitchen. Even those who possess a good level of *basic interpersonal communication skills (BICS)* have limited knowledge of academic language, what Cummins (2000) refers to as *cognitive academic language proficiency (CALP)*.

In science class, students are frequently required to conduct or read about experiments. The language in a textbook or lecture regarding an experiment uses general English words but relies heavily on scientific academic terms as well. Clearly, ELLs face a hurdle in attempting to understand this language in their texts and teacher lectures. In addition, their limited ability with this language affects science assessment in two ways. First, ELLs may take longer to read questions on exams, leaving less time to answer the questions. At the same time, ELLs have a difficult time writing answers that make use of the right vocabulary that a native-speaking teacher will recognize and score as appropriate in a science environment.

What can teachers do? Teachers should make every attempt to clarify their own presentations through simplified language and appropriate visuals. Although teachers are mainly concerned with the science curriculum, they should not avoid scientific terminology because that vocabulary is an integral part of the course objectives. Our mandate is to get across our content material as best we can for all learners, both native and non-native speakers. We can do this by modifying our delivery, not cutting back on content.

When assessing, teachers should be aware that the language in exam questions can obscure the actual meaning of the question. This language is particularly important in two of the most common question types on science tests, namely multiple choice and extended answer questions.

Multiple Choice Questions in Science Assessment

To be sure, multiple choice questions are a valid type of question, but if students do not know certain words in the question and/or the answer choices, the validity of the question is in doubt. As was the case with the math word problem examples earlier in this chapter, the language in a question can prevent non-native learners from answering the question correctly, even when they actually know the scientific principle. The following two examples illustrate language problems for ESL students in multiple choice questions.

Science Question 1

A student wants to find out which kind of soil can hold the most water. She buys four identical pots with small holes in the bottom of each. She then fills each pot with a different kind of soil and waters the pots with the exact same amount of water. How can she determine the amount of water that stays in the soil in each pot?

    A. By putting cotton in each pot to see how much water it absorbs.

    B. By carefully examining the growth of flowers in each of the pots.

    C. By covering only three of the pots with a plastic bag.

    D. By measuring how much water drains from each pot.

Comments on Science Question 1

ESL students may know the scientific principle being assessed in this question, but they may not be able to answer this particular question because they do not know one or more of these vocabulary items: *find out, kind of* (meaning "type," not "nice" and not "sort of"), *soil, hold* (not "hold" as in *hold my hand* or *hold the baby;* in this example, no one is actually holding anything), *water* (as a verb, not the noun), *exact, determine,* and *amount.*

Even if the ELL understands the question, which is not a given, the four answer options include difficult vocabulary: *cotton, absorb, growth, cover, measure, drain.* For the ELL, the answer is D—unfortunately. We say *unfortunately* here because of all the words in the four answer options, the verb *drain* is probably the least known. (Again, note that some ELLs may know *drain* as a noun, a common item in every house, but this does not indicate knowledge of drain as a verb.) Without knowing the word *drain*, students cannot answer this question correctly—even if they know the scientific principle being tested by the question.

Science Question 2

Which of the following objects would have the most inertia?

    A. a pebble

    B. a boulder

    C. a soccer ball

    D. a head of cauliflower

    E. an empty garbage can

Comments on Science Question 2

Most teachers might think that the word that unfairly skews this assessment of science knowledge is *inertia*. However, that assumption is incorrect. The sole purpose of this question is to test students' ability to apply their knowledge of the concept of inertia to real-world items. Both the concept and the word *inertia* were covered in class; this was a primary objective of this particular science unit. Thus, testing about inertia is not only fair, it is a good teacher's obligation.

The unintentional but nonetheless unfair influence for ELLs lies in the five answer choices. While *soccer ball* and *empty garbage can* are probably known terms, students may or may not know *cauliflower* but are unlikely to understand what a head of cauliflower is (though they know the word *head*). ESL learners are highly unlikely to know what a *pebble* or a *boulder* is since these words are not very frequent in English. A more fair multiple choice question on students' ability to apply their knowledge of the term *inertia* would make use of answer choices that the teacher believes all students are likely to know, e.g., a bowling ball, a tennis ball, a basketball, a baseball, a golf ball. (The correct answer is *bowling ball.*)

Extended Answer Questions in Science Assessment

Extended answer questions confound ELLs on several levels. First, ELLs may not know key vocabulary in the question, which then impedes or prevents them from demonstrating their science knowledge. Second, ELLs' ability to write out an extended answer is usually limited. Their writing contains numerous grammatical and lexical mistakes, and these mistakes may cause the teacher—directly or indirectly—to award a lower score for an answer even though the answer is correct in terms of science information. Finally, extended questions in science often require students to analyze, compare, explain, or classify. ESL learners (and native speakers) may be accustomed to extended writing for a different purpose (e.g., reporting or narrating) and therefore lose points because they have not followed the proper rhetorical mode for science. In other words, they may report rather than analyze, which would most likely result in a lower score in a science assessment.

The following two examples illustrate language problems for ESL students in extended answer questions.

Science Question 3

The planet Saturn is about 34 times larger than the Earth's moon, but Saturn appears to be smaller than the moon when viewed from the Earth. Why is this?

Comments on Science Question 3

The relatively simple language of this question aids the ESL learner (and native speaker) to comprehend the question in two ways. First, when this concept was taught in class, the teacher probably talked about the size of the planets. Thus, difficult linguistic structures to express comparison such as "X is (number) times larger/smaller than Y" or "X is larger/smaller than Y" were probably used in class. A good ESL-trained teacher would have highlighted these structures when teaching the science lesson since the teacher's goal is proficiency in not only science but also English language. Second, the teacher broke the question down into two pieces: the content and then the actual question. One long question would have been much more difficult for an ESL learner to comprehend: *Why is it that the planet Saturn, which is about 34 times larger than the Earth's moon, appears to be smaller than the moon when viewed from the earth?* Because the actual question *Why is this?* is separate, the student is more likely to provide the reason rather than address some unrelated aspect of the question. In other words, the question is clear.

The difficult part of this question is not the language in the question but rather the language in the <u>answer</u>. Correct answers to this question include "Because Saturn is farther away from the Earth" or "The moon is closer to the Earth." In almost all correct answers to this question, the ESL student needs to be able to express a comparison, a rather difficult linguistic rule in English to use correctly. Single-syllable adjectives add the suffix *-er (bigger, smaller, denser)*, but adjectives of two or more syllables employ *more (more distant, more shallow, more extensive)*. However, two-syllable adjectives that end in *-y* add *-er*, not *more (heavier, saltier, rockier)*. As with all rules, there are a few exceptions *(farther, better, worse)*.

An answer with language errors that decrease or impede comprehension will almost certainly result in a lower score—even if the ELL knows the answer. One solution here is to make sure during teaching to present and practice comparative forms within an appropriate science context, i.e., teach language based on K–12 content needs. Again, only a teacher who has had some ESL training is even aware of these ESL language problems.

Science Question 4

A two-inch lit candle is placed in each of three glass jars. The candles are identical. Jar 1 is seven inches high. Jar 2 is five inches. Jar 3 is three inches high. Lids are placed on jars 2 and 3 but not on jar 1. Explain the order in which the candles will burn out.

Comments on Science Question 4

Key vocabulary in this question can be difficult for ESL learners and therefore impede or prevent them from demonstrating their knowledge of the interaction between the longevity of fire and the amount of oxygen surrounding it. Potentially problematic words include *lit, candle, place* (the verb, not the more common noun), *jar, order* ("sequence," not a restaurant request), and *burn out* (versus *burn*, which may be its antonym).

This question could be improved in two ways. First, the teacher could make sure to include words that were either covered in the science lesson or words that she believes the students are likely to know. Second, instead of asking this question in prose, the teacher could use illustrations as in this version of Science Question 4:

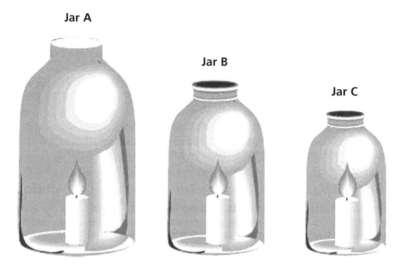

Jar A

Jar B

Jar C

Which candle will burn out first? ___
Which will be second? ___
Which will be last? ___
Explain your answers.

Ten Things to Remember about Assessing Content with K-12 ESL Students

1. **Most states or school districts have legal mandates to allow accommodations for ESL learners when they take tests.**
   Though these accommodations vary from state to state, some of the more common ones include:
   - allowing more time for the test
   - allowing the use of a bilingual dictionary
   - allowing an aide to read the test to the student
   - modifying the language in the question

2. **Make sure that the language in the exam is language that ELLs know.**
   For example, teach content-specific terms such as *take away* or *times* for math or *dissect* or *trace* for science. A basic tenet of assessment is that assessment begins in the class planning stage; it is not tacked on haphazardly at the end of instruction. Thus, as you plan your lessons, think of ELLs' language issues and needs.

3. **Take into account ELLs' problems with writing.**
   Consider how writing extended answers can lower ESL students' scores. You may wish to give two scores: one for content and one for language expression.

4. **Provide models of correct answers in class.**
   This does not mean teaching to the test; instead, it means explicitly teaching students how to answer a question that requires them to analyze or compare. This will benefit both native speakers and ELLs.

5. **Break longer questions into smaller chunks.**
   In longer questions, state the exact task (e.g., Explain the 5 steps in germination) separately.

6. **For at least part of the overall picture of student achievement, consider alternative assessments rather than traditional pen-and-paper tests.**
   Alternatives for math could include having students work out a word problem at your desk, explaining orally every step in the process. Alternatives for science might include a science project that all students present to the class, explaining their research question, their procedures, their results, and their conclusions or implications based on their results.

7. **For completion (i.e., fill in the blanks) questions, provide a word bank for vocabulary purposes.**

8. **In review sessions in class, have ESL students work with native-speaking students as they go over possible answers.**
   Not only does this pairing potentially help the ESL learner with the language to answer this particular question, it also serves as a significant opportunity for comprehensible input (Krashen, 1985) and pushed output (Swain, 1993), both of which are important for the acquisition of a second language.

9. **We must make sure we assess students' knowledge of the content area and not their cultural knowledge or awareness. Avoid questions that have culturally specific items that ESL learners might not be able to relate to.**

10. **Make sure that your tests cover material that was presented in class and that they test in a similar manner in which the material was taught.**
    For example, if you had students explain a scientific process orally in small groups, do not test this knowledge by having them write it out individually on a test. Remember: Good assessment matches good teaching.

Extension Activity

Here is a science test that Mr. Knott developed. Look at the test from the perspective of an ESL teacher and then read Ms. Wright's review of the test.

5th Grade Science Test   Name _____

Part 1. Multiple Choice. (20%; 4 points each)

1. To the average person, one obvious difference between oak trees and pine trees is
   A. their leaves
   B. their cell structure
   C. their ability to store water
   D. the kinds of seeds that each produces

2. Along most coasts, tides usually occur twice
   A. daily
   B. weekly
   C. monthly
   D. yearly

3. Clearing a forest to build a shopping center will most likely cause woodpeckers to
   A. lay more eggs
   B. build smaller nests
   C. seek a new habitat
   D. fly at higher altitudes

4. Mr. Jones planted some bushes along the walkway in front of his house. The bushes that were close to the street had more blooms than the bushes that were close to the house. Which statement is a hypothesis that Mr. Jones could make about this situation?
   A. The bushes near the house had fewer blooms and leaves.
   B. The bushes near the house were taller but had fewer blooms.
   C. There were many blooms on the bushes near the house and fewer blooms on the bushes next to the street.
   D. The bushes next to the street had more blooms because they received more sunlight.

5. Why is it that if you drag your feet across a carpet and then touch a doorknob, you will get shocked?
   A. environmental shock
   B. static electricity
   C. gravity shock
   D. carpet electricity

Part 2. Extended answer. (80%)
Answer <u>one</u> of these questions. You may select which question you want to answer.

1. Explain the relationship between animal life and plant life.
2. Many plants and animals have adapted to the environment in which they live. List 5 examples. For each example, explain how the plant or animal has adapted.

Ms. Wright's Comments on the Science Test

Two strengths of this exam are that you have included different kinds of questions and you gave students a choice with some questions. The different kinds of questions address ELLs' language needs. Your multiple choice questions do not require language production. Allowing students to choose which question they want to answer in Part 2 helps both ELLs and native speakers alike in that they can select the question they know more content about and have better language expression ability.

However, a careful analysis of the questions reveals these problems:

1. Question 1 is a fair question. We can safely assume that the difficult words in this question are science words that were covered in the text and in class lectures.
2. Question 2 is a fair question. In fact, you added the phrase "along most coasts" even though this phrase is not necessary.
3. In question 3, will students know *clear* (as a verb, not an adjective with a positive meaning), *likely*, *woodpeckers*, and *nests*? Perhaps the most problematic word is *woodpecker*. Why not just use the more common word *bird*? It is more familiar to students and still allows you to test the science principle.
4. In question 4, adding an illustration would be helpful. Will students know *walkway*, *bushes*, *close to* (vs. *to close*), *blooms*, and *fewer*?
5. In question 5, will students know *drag*, *carpet*, and *doorknob*?

6. A larger problem is that a whopping 80 percent of the exam depends on one question. This is a violation of good testing. In addition, it places an enormous burden on ELLs' productive language skills. Surely, ELLs and native speakers with weak spelling or language ability will be penalized. (By the way, do you have a rubric already made out for scoring the extended answer question? Does your rubric allocate more weight to content than to language?)

7. You need more multiple choice questions; a total of five questions is not sufficient. Consider adding some questions that are easy and some that are difficult. Right now most of the questions seem to be at about the same degree of difficulty.

8. It is certainly good that you gave your students the opportunity to choose which of the two extended answer questions they want to answer. This benefits both native speakers and ELLs in that they can choose the question for which they know more content information and have more language expression ability. However, these two questions are not at all equivalent. The first question, *Explain the relationship between animal life and plant life* is too vague. What do you want them to mention here? You should list at least some of the areas that you want your students to address in their answers. The second question is better because it enumerates which information you want by asking students to list 5 examples and then to explain how each has adapted. This question is much clearer. In addition, the second question is better because you have broken this long question into three parts: background + task + task. Again, this division aids not only ELLs but also your native-speaking students.

Appendix: Standardized ESL/EFL Tests

Name of Test	Test Producer	Test Description	Test Purpose
American Council on the Teaching of Foreign Languages Oral Proficiency Interview (ACTFL OPI)	American Council on the Teaching of Foreign Languages *www.actfl.org/i4a/ pages/index.cfm? pageid=3348*	Face-to-face oral or telephone interview between a certified examiner and examinee; measures candidates against ten ability levels from novice low to superior	A standardized oral proficiency assessment designed to test functional speaking ability
Basic English Skills Test Plus (BEST Plus™)	Center for Applied Linguistics *www.cal.org/topics/ ta/best.html*	Takes the place of the BEST; an oral proficiency interview that assesses listening comprehension, language complexity, and communication	Designed to assess Adult English language proficiency
Basic English Skills Test Literacy Skills (BEST Literacy™)	Center for Applied Linguistics *www.cal.org/topics/ ta/best.html*	A companion test to the BEST Plus™ oral proficiency interview	Designed to assess Adult English language proficiency
Canadian Academic English Language Assessment (CAEL)	Carleton University *www.cael.ca*	Measures EAP in the four skills (reading, writing, listening, speaking)	Designed to evaluate English in use for EAP programs; verifies whether a student's level of English proficiency is adequate for university study.
Comprehensive English Language Learning Assessment (CELLA)	Educational Testing Services *www.ets.org*	A four-skills language proficiency assessment	Designed to provide evidence of program accountability in accordance with Title III No Child Left Behind and information about students' strengths and weaknesses.

Name of Test	Test Producer	Test Description	Test Purpose
Certificate in Advanced English (CAE)	University of Cambridge ESOL Examinations *http://cambridgeesol. org/exams/cae.htm*	Consists of five sections (Reading, Writing, Use of English, Listening, Speaking); each component is worth 20% of the overall score; administered and graded by trained examiners.	An advanced-level exam intended for those who want to work/study abroad or develop a career that requires language skills; 2nd highest level of Cambridge ESOL exams at level C1 of Council of Europe's Common European Framework (CEF)
Certificate of Proficiency in English (CPE)	University of Cambridge ESOL Examinations *http://cambridgesol. org/exams/cpe.htm*	Consists of five sections (Reading, Writing, Use of English, Listening, Speaking); each component is worth 20% of the overall score; administered and graded by trained examiners.	An advanced-level exam designed for those already advanced in English and/or are approaching the standard of an educated native speaker of English; highest level of Cambridge ESOL exams at level C2 of Council of Europe's CEF.
Comprehensive Adult Student Assessment System (CASAS)	CASAS, Foundation for Educational Achievement *www.casas.org*	Consists of listening and reading comprehension sections with the writing and speaking sections as optional components	Assesses vocational preparation, workplace literacy, and adult basic education
First Certificate in English (FCE)	University of Cambridge ESOL Examinations *http://cambridgesol. org/exams/fce.htm*	Consists of five sections (Reading, Writing, Use of English, Listening, Speaking); each component is worth 20% of the overall score; administered and graded by trained examiners.	An intermediate-level exam for those who want to work/study abroad or develop a career that requires language skills; Cambridge ESOL exams at level B2 of Council of Europe's CEF.

Name of Test	Test Producer	Test Description	Test Purpose
International Baccalaureate English B Component (IBO)	International Baccalaureate Organization *www.ibo.org*	The ESL/EFL component of the International Baccalaureate program; consists of an oral internal assessment and two written sections (one measures reading comprehension/ related skills; the second measures writing ability).	Assesses whether students have met the exit requirements for the International Baccalaureate certificate.
International English Language Testing System (IELTS™)	British Council, IDP Australia, and University of Cambridge ESOL Examinations *www.ielts.org*	Four skills exam; two modules (General and Academic); administered and graded by trained examiners.	Measures the ability to communicate in English across four language skill areas (listening, reading, writing, speaking); intended for people who want to study or work in Anglophone speaking countries.
Key English Test (KET)	*University of Cambridge ESOL Examinations http://cambridgesol. org/exams/ket.htm*	Four skills exam with three sections (Reading & Writing, Listening, Speaking); each skill is worth 25% of overall score; administered and graded by trained examiners	An elementary exam testing students' ability to deal with basic written and spoken communications; 1st level of Cambridge ESOL exams at level A2 of Council of Europe's CEF.
Michigan English Language Assessment Battery (MELAB)	University of Michigan English Language Institute *www.lsa.umich.edu/ eli/testing/melab/*	Contains three sections (Writing, Listening Comprehension, and Grammar/Cloze/Reading/Vocabulary); a Speaking test is optional	A standardized English language proficiency test used to evaluate English language competence of adult language learners of English.

Name of Test	Test Producer	Test Description	Test Purpose
Preliminary English Test (PET)	University of Cambridge ESOL Examinations *http://cambridgesol. org/exams/pet.htm*	Four skills exam with three sections (Reading & Writing, Listening, Speaking); each skill is worth 25% of overall score; administered and graded by trained examiners.	An intermediate-level exam testing students' ability to cope with everyday written and spoken communications; 2nd level of Cambridge ESOL exams at level B1 of Council of Europe's CEF.
Secondary Level English Proficiency Test (SLEP®)	Educational Testing Services *www.toefl.org/ educator//edslep.html*	Consists of a listening and a reading section	Measures general ability in understanding spoken and written English for international students in U.S. secondary schools; sometimes used in post-secondary institutions outside the U.S.
Test of English as a Foreign Language (TOEFL®) • TOEFL® ITP • CBT • PBT • iBT	Educational Testing Services *www.ets.org*	Offered in different formats depending on a student's location (i.e., institutional, paper-based, computer-based, iBT); assesses all four language skills; marked by trained examiners.	Measures the ability of non-native speakers of English to use and understand English in North American academic contexts.
Test of English for International Communication (TOEIC®) or TOEIC® Bridge	Educational Testing Services *www.toeic.org*	MCQ exam divided into two sections (Listening Comprehension and Reading)	Measures and certifies listening, reading, and grammatical proficiency in international business English at both intermediate and advanced levels; TOEIC® Bridge, primarily diagnostic, is designed for beginning and intermediate learners of English.

Name of Test	Test Producer	Test Description	Test Purpose
Test of Spoken English (TSE®) TOEFL® Academic Speaking Test (TAST®) Speaking Proficiency English Assessment Kit (SPEAK®)	Educational Testing Services *www.ets.org/tse*	Semi-direct test that requires students to respond to a variety of text-based or audio prompts; presented and recorded on audiotape; consists of four sections; audiotapes are graded by two examiners; the TSE® is an official test that can be used for admissions or certification; TAST® is a subset of the TOEFL® iBT's new speaking portion; SPEAK® tests are retired forms of TSE® exams.	A high-stakes test of general English language spoken proficiency used in North American universities to make decisions about a student's ability to communicate in an academic context.

References

Alderson, J. C. (2000). *Assessing reading.* Cambridge: Cambridge University Press.

Alderson, J. C., & Bachman, L. (2001). Series editors' preface. In G. Buck, *Assessing listening* (pp. x–xi). Cambridge: Cambridge University Press.

Alderson, J. C., Clapham, C., & Wall, D. (1995). *Language test construction and evaluation.* Cambridge: Cambridge University Press.

Bachman, L. (1990). *Fundamental considerations in language testing.* Oxford: Oxford University Press.

Bachman, L., & Palmer, A. (1996). *Language testing in practice.* Oxford: Oxford University Press.

Blau, E. (1991). The effect of syntax, speed and pauses on listening comprehension. *TESOL Quarterly, 24,* 46–53.

Bloom, B. (1984). *Taxonomy of educational objectives.* Boston: Pearson Education.

Brindley, G. (1989). *Assessment achievements in the learner-centered curriculum.* Sydney: National Centre for English Language Teaching and Research, MacQuarie University.

Brown, G., & Yule, G. (1983). *Teaching the spoken language: An approach based on the analysis of conversational English.* New York: Cambridge University Press.

Brown, H. D. (1994). *Principles of language learning and teaching.* Englewood Cliffs, NJ: Prentice Hall.

———. (2004). *Language assessment: Principles and classroom practices.* White Plains, NY: Longman.

Brown, J. D. (2005). *Testing in language programs: A comprehensive guide to English language assessment.* New York: McGraw Hill.

Buck, G. (2001). *Assessing listening.* Cambridge: Cambridge University Press.

Canale, M. (1984). Considerations in the testing of reading and listening proficiency. *Foreign Language Annals, 17,* 349–357.

Canale, M., & Swain, M. (1980). Theoretical bases of communicative approaches to second language teaching and testing. *Applied Linguistics, 1,* 1–47.

Carroll, J. B. (1972). Fundamental considerations in testing for English language proficiency of foreign students. In H. B. Allen & R. N. Campbell (Eds.), *Teaching English as a second language: A book of readings.* New York: McGraw Hill.

Cohen, A. (1994). *Assessing language ability in the classroom.* Boston: Heinle & Heinle.

Cummins, J. (2000). *Language, power and pedagogy: Bilingual children in the crossfire.* Clevedon, UK: Multilingual Matters.

Davidson, F., & Lynch, B. (2002). *Testcraft: A teacher's guide to writing and using language test specifications.* London: Yale University Press.

Davidson, P., & Lloyd, D. (2005). Guidelines for developing a reading test. In D. Lloyd, P. Davidson, & C. Coombe (Eds.), *The fundamentals of language assessment: A practical guide for teachers in the Gulf* (pp. 53–63). Dubai: TESOL Arabia Publications.

Davies, A., Brown, A., Elder, C., Hill, K., Lumley, T., & McNamara, T. (1999). *Dictionary of language testing.* Cambridge: Cambridge University Press.

Dickinson, L. (1987). *Self-instruction in language learning.* Cambridge: Cambridge University Press.

Ferris, D. R. (2002). *Treatment of error in second language student writing.* Ann Arbor: University of Michigan Press.

Flowerdew, J. (1994). Research of relevance to second language lecture comprehension: An overview. In J. Flowerdew (Ed.), *Academic listening: Research perspectives* (pp. 55–74). Cambridge: Cambridge University Press.

Folse, K. S. (1996). *Discussion starters: Speaking fluency activities for advanced ESL/EFL students.* Ann Arbor: University of Michigan Press.

———. (2004a). *Intermediate reading practices: Building reading and vocabulary skills* (3rd ed). Ann Arbor: University of Michigan Press.

———. (2004b). *Vocabulary myths: Applying second language research to classroom teaching.* Ann Arbor: University of Michigan Press.

———. (2006). *The art of teaching speaking: Research and pedagogy for the ESL/EFL classroom.* Ann Arbor: University of Michigan Press.

Folse, K., & Brummett, K. (2006). Pedagogical grammar courses offered by MATESOL programs in Florida. *Sunshine State TESOL Journal, 5*(1), 1–12.

Frary, R. B. (1995). *More multiple-choice item writing do's and don'ts.* (ERIC/AE Digest Series EDO-TM-95-4)

Genesee, F. 2001. Evaluation. In D. Nunan & R. Carter (Eds.), *The Cambridge guide to teaching English to speakers of other languages* (pp. 144–150). Cambridge: Cambridge University Press.

Hamp-Lyons, L. (1990a). Research on the rating process. *TESOL Quarterly, 29,* 4.

———. (1990b). Second language writing: Assessment issues. In B. Kroll (Ed.), *Second language writing: Research insights for the classroom* (pp. 69–87). New York: Cambridge University Press.

———. (1991). Scoring procedures for ESL contexts. In L. Hamp-Lyons (Ed.), *Assessing second language writing in academic contexts* (pp. 241–276). Norwood, NJ: Ablex.

Harris, D. (1977). *Testing English as a second language.* New York: McGraw-Hill.

Harris, M., & McCann, P. 1994. *Assessment.* Oxford: MacMillan Heinemann.

Harrison, A. (1983). *A language testing handbook.* New York: MacMillan.

Heaton, J. B. (1990). *Classroom testing.* Harlow, UK: Longman.

———. (1995). *Writing English language tests.* New York: Longman.

Henning, G. (1987). *A guide to language testing: Development, evaluation, research.* Boston: Newbury House.

Huerta-Macias, A. (1995). Alternative assessment: Answers to commonly asked questions. *TESOL Journal, 5,* 8–10.

Hughes, A. (2000). *Testing for language teachers.* Cambridge: Cambridge University Press.

———. (2003). *Testing for language teachers* (2nd ed). Cambridge: Cambridge University Press.

Hyland, F. (1998). The impact of teacher written feedback on individual writers. *Journal of Second Language Writing, 7*(3), 255–286.

Hyland, K. (2003). *Second language writing.* Cambridge: Cambridge University Press.

Iteman classical item analysis software. (2006). Assessment Systems Corporation. http://www.assess.com/xcart/home.php

Jacobs, H. L., Zinkgraf, S. A., Wormuth, D. R., Hartfiel, V. F., & Hughey, J. B. (1981). *Testing ESL composition: A practical approach.* Rowley, MA: Newbury House.

Jones, W. (2005). Assessing students' oral proficiency. In D. Lloyd, P. Davidson, & C. Coombe (Eds.), *The fundamentals of language assessment: A practical guide for teachers in the Gulf* (pp. 75–86). Dubai: TESOL Arabia Publications.

Kellerman, S. (1992). 'I see what you mean': The role of kinesic behavior in listening and implications for foreign and second language learning. *Applied Linguistics, 13,* 239–258.

Kindler, A. L. (2002). Survey of the states' Limited English Proficient students and available educational programs and services, 2000–2001 summary report. [Electronic version]. Washington, DC: National Clearinghouse for English Language Acquisition and Language Instruction Educational Programs. Retrieved October 3, 2005, from http://www.ncela.gwu.edu/policy/states/reports/seareports/0001/sea0001.pdf

Krashen, S. (1985). *The input hypothesis: Issues and implications.* New York: Longman.

Kroll, B., & Reid, J. (1994). Guidelines for designing writing prompts: Clarifications, caveats and cautions. *Journal of Second Language Writing, 3*(3), 231–255.

Leki, I. (1990). Coaching from the margins: Issues in written response. In B. Kroll (Ed.), *Second language writing: Insights from the language classroom* (pp. 57–68). Cambridge: Cambridge University Press.

MacDonald, V. (2004). *The status of English Language Learners in Florida: Trends and prospects.* Tempe, AZ: Education Policy Studies Laboratory of Arizona State University. EPSL-0401-113-EPRU

Markham, P. (1988). Gender differences and the perceived expertness of the speaker as factors in ESL listening recall. *TESOL Quarterly, 22,* 397–406.

Mazak, C., Zwier, L., & Stafford-Yilmaz, L. (2004). *The Michigan Guide to English for academic success and better TOEFL® test scores.* Ann Arbor: University of Michigan Press.

Nation, P. (1990). *Teaching and learning vocabulary.* Boston: Heinle & Heinle.

Nunan, D. (2002). Teaching listening. In J. C. Richards & W. A. Renandya (Eds.), *Methodology in language teaching: An anthology of current practice* (pp. 235–237). Cambridge: Cambridge University Press.

Oller, J. (1979). *Language tests at school: A pragmatic approach.* London: Longman.

O'Malley, J., & Valdez Pierce, L. (1996). *Authentic assessment for English Language Learners: Practical approaches for teachers.* Reading, MA: Addison-Wesley.

Oscarson, M. (1984). *Self-assessment of foreign language skills: A survey of research and development work.* Strasbourg: Council of Europe.

———. (1989) Self-assessment of language proficiency: Rationale and applications. In *Encyclopedia of language and education* (Vol. 7, pp. 1–13). Norwell, MA: Kluwer Publishing.

Paulson, F., Paulson, P., & Meyer, C. (1991). What makes a portfolio a portfolio? *Educational Leadership, 48*(5), 60–63.

Peyton, J. K., & Reed, L. (1990). *Dialogue journal writing with non-native English speakers: A handbook for teachers.* Alexandria, VA: TESOL.

Prator, C., & Robinett, B. W. (1972). *Manual of American English pronunciation.* New York: Holt, Rinehart and Winston.

Richards, J. (1983). Listening comprehension: Approach, design, procedure. *TESOL Quarterly, 17,* 219–239.

Rost, M. (1990). *Listening in language learning.* New York: Longman.

Santos, M. (1997). Portfolio assessment and the role of learner reflection. *English Language Teaching Forum, 35*(2), 10.

Scarcella, R. C., & Oxford, R. L. (1992). *The tapestry of language learning: The individual in the communicative classroom.* Boston: Heinle & Heinle.

Spellings, M. (2005, December). Opening address presented at the Celebrate Our Rising Stars Summit, Office of English Language Acquisition (OELA), Washington, DC.

Stebbins, C. (2002). A profile of Florida's bilingual paraprofessionals. *Sunshine State TESOL Journal, 1,* 35–42.

Swain, M. (1993). The output hypothesis: Just speaking and writing aren't enough. *The Canadian Modern Language Review, 50,* 158–164.

Tauroza, S. (1997). *Listening comprehension: How to teach it rather than test it.* Cairo: American University in Cairo Press.

Tauroza, S., & Allison, D. (1990). Speech rates in British English. *Applied Linguistics, 11,* 90–115.

Weir, Cyril. (1993). *Understanding and developing language tests.* Hertfordshire, UK: Prentice Hall.

Subject Index

academic dishonesty, 148–149, 153–154, 156

accommodations policy, 155, 172, 184

accountability, xiv, 13, 159, 168

achievement tests, xvii, xx; purpose of, xxi; timing of, xxi

administering assessment, 147–157; after the test, 152–154; before the test, 148–152; during the test, 152; issues in, 154–155

alternative assessment, xx, xix, 15, 18. *See also* learner-centered assessment, oral presentations, portfolio assessment, projects, self-assessment, student-designed tests

analysis, 11, 15; analysis software, 166; importance of, 3; purpose of, 158–160

analytical marking scale, 71, 83–84, 122–123

answer key, contruction of, 9–10, 15, 37, 153

aptitude tests, xvi, xxi

assessment, xiii, xv; process of, 4–12, 13

authenticity, xxv, xxvi, xxviii, 90, 94, 110. *See also* cornerstones of testing

background knowledge, 25, 29, 45, 93, 107

bell curve, 162

benchmark papers, 70, 80

bias, 23, 37, 51, 86

BICS (Basic Interpersonal Communication Skills), 179

bottom-up processing, 44, 91

calibration, 77, 80, 83, 86, 106, 129, 159

CALP (Cognitive Academic Language Proficiency), 179

CBT (computer-based testing), 10, 136, 140

cheating. *See* academic dishonesty

cloze/gap fill format, 33–34, 99–100; and cloze summary, 61–63; and fixed-ratio, 61, and rational deletion, 52

communicative approach, 91–92

construct, test, 5, 43, 45

content-based instruction, 69, 185

content knowledge: in mathematics, 174–178; in science, 178–184

cornerstones of testing, xxii, 107; violations of, xxviii–xxx. *See also* authenticity, practicality, reliability, security, transparency, usefulness, validity, washback

correction codes, 84–85

criterion-referenced assessment/tests, xviii, xx, 162

debate, 123–125

diagnostic assessment/tests, xiv, xvi; purpose of, xxi; timing of, xxi

dialogue journals, 78, 143

dictation, 100–101

distractors, 19, 24, 25, 26, 163, 165

distribution, 158, 160

double-blind marking, 84, 86

elicitation mode, 7–8

essay questions, 35–36; advantages/disadvantages of 35–36; tips for writing good questions, 36. *See also* extended answer questions

ETS (Educational Testing Service), xvii, 81

extemporaneous speaking, 126. *See also* impromptu speaking

of, 27–28; format of, 27; tips for writing good items, 29–31

usefulness (of a test), xxii. *See also* cornerstones of testing

validity, xxii, 133, 159; construct validity, xxii, xxviii; content validity, xxii, xxvi, 185; face validity, xxii, xxviii. *See also* cornerstones of testing

vocabulary, 46, 94–95; content-specific terms, 185; explicit instruction, 46; general vocabulary, 179; incidental learning, 46; limited ELL, 172–197; technical vocabulary, 179, 182; vocabulary notebook, 135; vocabulary profiler, 94–95; word bank, 185; word problems, 176–177

washback, xxiv, xxv, xxix, 46, 129, 144, 146, 167, 168. *See also* cornerstones of testing

word problems, in assessing content knowledge, 174–177

writing assessment: approaches to, 71; designing assessment tasks, 71–75; issues in, 75–76; marking procedures for, 80; scales, 80–84; techniques for, 76–79

Author Index